Museum of Childhood

A Book of Childhood Things

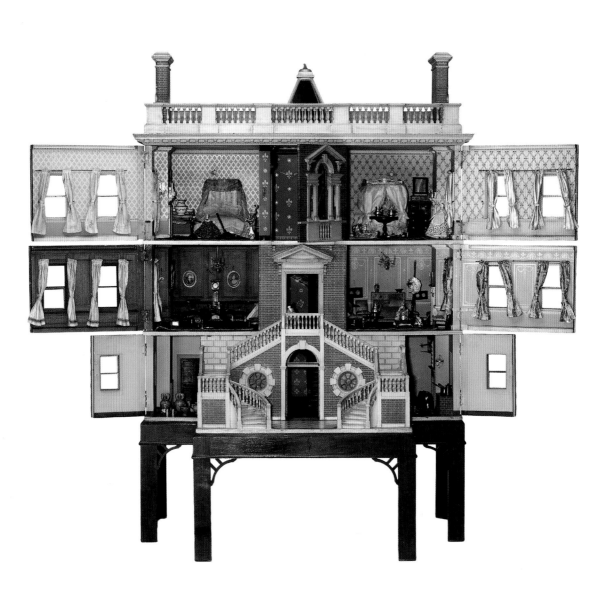

A Book of Childhood Things

Sarah Wood

V&A Publishing

First published by V&A Publishing, 2012
Victoria and Albert Museum
South Kensington
London SW7 2RL
www.vandabooks.com

ISBN 9781 85177 703 7

10 9 8 7 6 5 4 3 2 1
2016 2015 2014 2013 2012

Design: hikedesign.co.uk
Copy-editor: Rachel Malig

V&A photography by V&A Photographic Studio
Page 6 (bottom): © Peter Durant

Printed in Italy

Cover: Space Hopper (p.108), bath toy (p.34), plimsolls (p.69), alphabet blocks (p.80), Eames
Elephant (p.35), dolls' house (p.74), pin cushion doll (p.43), mechanical tin beetle (p.98),
rocking horse (p.14); back cover: dress (p.20), silver rattle (p.30), highchair (p.13), Union Jack
nappy (p.35), Rubik's Cube (p.21), teddy bear (p.100); front flap: Grenadier Guards (p.99); page 2:
Tate Baby House (p.93)

V&A Publishing
Supporting the world's leading
museum of art and design,
the Victoria and Albert
Museum, London

Childhood is one of the few life experiences that we all share. At the Museum of Childhood we are passionate about the importance of childhood and its crucial role in our development as human beings; it deserves to be explored in all its facets: fun, rich, complex and poignant.

The Museum of Childhood is in Bethnal Green, East London, and forms a branch of the Victoria and Albert Museum. It is arguably the most prestigious of its kind in the world, and aims to celebrate and explore the many themes of childhood, past and present. It contains Great Britain's finest and biggest childhood collection, including games, toys, children's clothing, furniture and ephemera. This book introduces the collection, and shows some of its most iconic pieces.

Rhian Harris, Director
Museum of Childhood

LEGO FAMILY
Manufactured by Lego
Denmark, 1970s
V&A: B.66-2004

See also pp.104, 112

INTRODUCTION

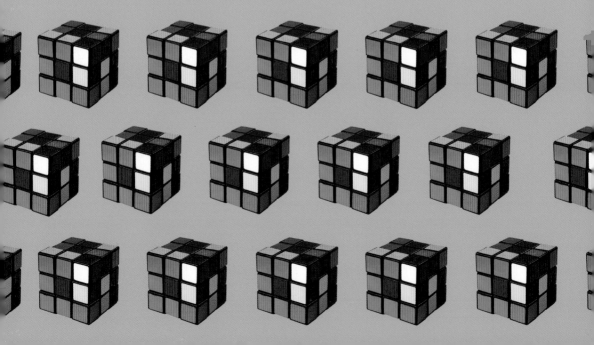

The Museum has occupied its site in Bethnal Green since 1872, although it was not until 1974, over 100 years later, that it became a museum of childhood. The building's architecture and its changing purpose as a museum has a history as fascinating as the objects that are contained within it.

The Museum's original wrought-iron framework came to Bethnal Green as a second-hand building. In 1864, the expansion of the South Kensington Museum (which had by then been renamed the Victoria and Albert Museum) necessitated an improved and permanent structure; the temporary triple-arched iron structure that had been erected was no longer seen as suitable, and due to its ugly, utilitarian design had earned it the unfavourable nickname of the Brompton Boilers. As plans developed for improved buildings at South Kensington, the structure of the Boilers was dismantled and offered in sections to different London authorities in order to construct new district museums. Bethnal Green was chosen as the East London site, and was the only one of the district museums to eventually go ahead.

In 1868 the framework of the building was transferred to Bethnal Green and, with the architectural guidance of J.W. Wild, work began on converting this bare iron structure into a new museum for the East End. Original plans for the Bethnal Green Museum, published in *The Builder* in 1871, included a brick exterior structure constructed around the iron framework. There were also plans for a series of extensions that were never built, including a curator's residence, a library and a large clock tower.

Projects that did go ahead included beautiful murals designed by F.W. Moody for the exterior of the brick building; these depicted scenes of art, industry and agriculture, the central themes for the Museum's intended displays. Inside the Museum the structure has changed little since it was first built and comprises one large open plan space with galleries running around a first and mezzanine floors. On the ground level the black and white patterned mosaic marble floor created and laid by female inmates of Woking Gaol, a prison for convicts with mental or physical disabilities, is still visible today in the heart of the building.

The Museum's most recent architectural additions were completed in 2006 by architects Caruso St John. They created a new front extension, including the Front Room, a gallery space intended to engage visitors with childhood through the Museum's collection and artist- and community-led projects and displays.

Constructing the Boilers at South Kensington, April 1856

The arrival of the Prince of Wales at the Bethnal Green Museum, 24 June 1872

The Prince of Wales opening the Bethnal Green Museum, 24 June 1872

Museum of Childhood

The original plan for the Museum by J.W. Wild, 1871

THE EARLY COLLECTION

The Bethnal Green Museum was opened by the Prince of Wales on 24 June 1872. At the beginning of its life, the Museum comprised Art and Science collections, and a selection of food and animal products previously on display at South Kensington. It also became a temporary home for other collections, notably Richard Wallace's eighteenth-century French art collection, before it found a permanent home at Manchester Square in central London.

Although the museum at Bethnal Green did not formally become a museum of childhood until 1974, from the 1920s onwards there was a concerted effort to consider the content and interpretation of the displays in terms of children. In 1922 Arthur Sabin was appointed Curator of the Museum. Following on from ideas realized in a successful children's exhibition at the V&A in 1915, Sabin developed his own plan for Bethnal Green. His main vision was to make all displays accessible for children and to develop a collection relating to childhood. Sabin instructed that paintings were hung at a low level in order for children to be able to view them with ease. He also set up classrooms and employed teachers to educate his young visitors.

In 1923 Sabin set up Bethnal Green's own successful children's exhibition and went on to develop a permanent children's section at the Museum. Alongside established displays, Sabin developed a toy collection that was supported by significant donations from Queen Mary, a patron of the Museum, and other collectors such as Mrs Greg of Leeds and Mrs Walter Tate. These gifts laid the foundations for the Museum's future collections.

In 1974, under the directorship of Roy Strong, the Bethnal Green Museum was officially launched as a museum of childhood, marking its advancement from a simple collection of toys, to a collection that represented the history and culture of childhood, broader than that of any comparable institution. Non-relevant collections were returned to the main V&A site in South Kensington, and a significant number of childhood-related objects were transferred to Bethnal Green from other Museum departments, including furniture, fashion and textile, and metalwork.

The collection comprises a wealth of objects representing the last 300 years of childhood. Much more than just toys, the collection documents and celebrates the material culture created around childhood, from the finery of royal children's clothing to the cheapest homemade plaything.

The reality of which objects have survived, been kept, purchased by and donated to the Museum has had a bearing on which representations of past childhoods are possible. Much of the collection can be seen as reflective of the power of the Industrial Revolution and the rise of consumerism within the newly acknowledged 'middle classes' from the eighteenth century onwards. There are also objects that highlight issues and problems faced by children in the past, such as poverty, education, work and illness.

Since the 1970s, the collection has grown considerably, and includes internationally significant examples of dolls' houses, dolls, toys, furniture, costume, childcare equipment, ephemera, archives and other items.

This book introduces the Museum's collection, following some of the broader themes of childhood, and documents children's lives through art and design artefacts. Together, these objects can give us an insight into how children from different backgrounds and different eras might have lived, thought and felt.

HIGHCHAIR
Designed by Gerrit Thomas Rietveld
Produced by G.A. Van Der Groenekan
The Netherlands, 1960s
V&A: B.1–2008

See also pp.25, 34

Mr F. Wilson, guide lecturer, teaching a school party, 1926

ROCKING HORSE
England, 1605–8
V&A: B.1–2006

This seventeenth-century rocking horse is thought to be the earliest surviving example from England, probably dating from 1605–8. The body has been carved from a single piece of elm but, over time, sections of the head have been damaged and are now missing.

The horse has been linked to the young Charles I (1600–49), the second son of James VI of Scotland (James I in England). Accounts of Charles as a boy suggest he was a delicate child with speech and mobility problems. The household accounts list a type of wheelchair that was made for him, and it is recorded that he was still unable to walk at the age of five, with subsequent years spent undergoing treatment for what is now thought to have been rickets. The rocking horse may well have provided Charles with exercise and a method for strengthening his legs. By his tenth birthday, Charles's mobility was much improved and he was able to walk, ride, dance and play tennis. See also p.98

GIRL'S GOWN
England, c.1760
V&A: T.183–1965

This girl's gown was transferred to the Museum of Childhood from the V&A's textile department in 1979. Clothing from the eighteenth century tended to be formal and rich in appearance. Even poor people dressed in this formal style by buying garments that had once been of good quality, but which had become dirty or ragged over time. The sumptuous embroidered silk fabric came from China and would have been extremely expensive; it may even have been considered too valuable to use to make a child's dress when it was new. Its decoration includes butterflies, birds and vases in coloured silk threads, all hand-embroidered.

The silk's luxurious finish and the dressmaker's skill disguise the fact that there was not really enough fabric to make the dress. The bodice and sleeves use the colourful motifs to maximum decorative effect, but the skirt is made of the remaining pieces joined together – even though they don't match. See also pp.54, 56

Painted by Henriette Brown
Oil on canvas
France, 1860–80
V&A: 1083–1886

This painting is part of a large bequest of drawings, watercolours and oil paintings left to the Museum by Joshua Dixon (1811–85) in 1886. Later, the non-childhood related paintings were transferred to the main V&A site at South Kensington. *A Girl Writing* has become one of the most popular images in the collection and has been reproduced many times, perhaps because of its sentimental feel, popular in paintings of the late nineteenth century. See also p.40

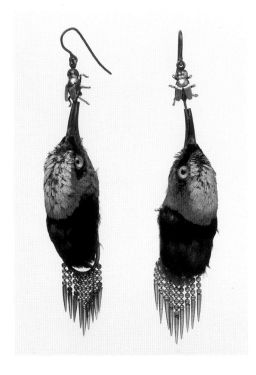

EARRINGS
England, c.1875
V&A: AP.258–1875

The exotic blue creeper birds used to make these earrings were popularly traded and used as ornamentation, particularly for women's headwear, in the Victorian period (1837–1901). They are from the Museum's collection of animal products, originally displayed when the Museum opened in 1872. Although using birds and animals for clothing and jewellery is less popular now, these earrings were made when affluent people showed their wealth by wearing lavishly ornate, rare, exotic and vibrant goods. Similar flora and fauna specimens were brought back from travel overseas and were among the types of object displayed at the Great Exhibition of 1851.

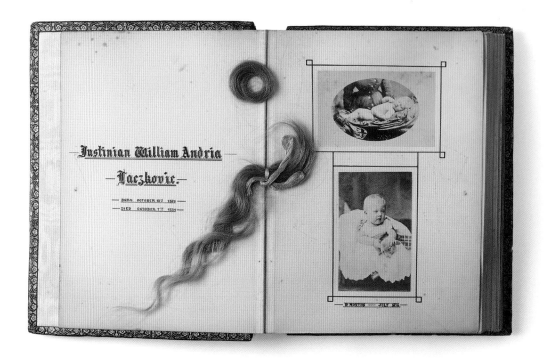

PHOTOGRAPH ALBUM
United Kingdom, 1875–84
V&A: B.82–1995

This photograph album records family customs and key moments from the short life of Justinian William Andria Laczkovic, from his birth on 18 October 1874 to his death from croup shortly before his tenth birthday on 7 October 1884. In the late nineteenth century the absence of modern medicine and nutrition meant that children were not always expected to reach adulthood. Justinian died while he was away at school, Christ's Hospital in Hertford, and his body would have been brought home for burial already in a coffin, although, unusually for the time, there is no photograph of Justinian laid out ready to be buried.

This opening page includes a lock of Justinian's hair, a tradition typical in Victorian mourning. See also p.42

AMY MILES' DOLLS' HOUSE
England, 1890
V&A: W.146–1921

This house was lent to the V&A for an exhibition in the Children's Room in 1915 and then given to the Museum in 1921. It was specifically made for a young girl, Amy Miles, in 1890. Dolls' houses were originally made by specialist craftsmen for the amusement of adults. This house would have been an extremely lavish plaything even for a wealthy family, not least because of its large size and high level of craftsmanship, and the hundreds of accessories it has been furnished with.

Amy's house gives a strong sense of late Victorian life, with gendered spaces such as the male billiard room, servants' quarters and designated children's areas, and reflects technological advances such as a geyser for heating the bath water.

Since the Industrial Revolution, dolls' houses have developed from bespoke items into mass-manufactured products used as adult and children's playthings. See also pp.2, 74, 93

PRINCESS DAISY DOLL AND LAYETTE
England and The Netherlands, 1890
V&A: Misc.88&89–1965

Princess Daisy is among a large number of royal bequests to the Museum, having been donated by Princess Mary in 1965. A Mrs Grothe Twiss from The Netherlands organized for this ordinary, mail-ordered English wax doll to have a lavish 176-piece layette (a collection of clothing and other objects considered essential for a newborn baby) handmade and exhibited to raise money for poor children. The doll was displayed and then raffled at the Amsterdam International Exhibition in 1895. With its accompanying layette, including personalized jewellery, the doll would have been a spectacular sight, and with such attention to detail and quality was a highly desirable prize. Nobody ever came forward to claim her from the raffle, and after a similar fundraising process in England, the doll was eventually given as a gift to Princess Mary, the daughter of Queen Mary, who gave her to the Museum. See also pp.44, 92, 97, 102

CATTLEY TOYS AND WATERCOLOUR
Watercolour by Constance Cattley
England, 1890–1910
V&A: Misc.57-78-1979

Gilbert, Nellie, Constance, Maud and Donald
Cattley were all born between 1885 and
1892, and between them owned these toys.
Some are handmade, such as Pumpie the
Elephant, and some are early examples of
manufactured teddy bears and toys. The
toys were treated as part of the family, and
the children made them beautiful clothes,
wrote stories, took photographs and painted
pictures of them.

This watercolour by Constance Cattley
features some of their toy family, including
Tommy, Baby, Pumpie and Polly. See also
pp.49, 64, 100, 111

SUSANNE AND ILSE GOTTSCHALK
Painted by Joseph Oppenheimer
Germany, 1933
V&A: B.49-51–2004

Sisters Susanne and Ilse Gottschalk were from a German Jewish family, who fled to a new life in Britain following the rise of the Nazi party in the 1930s. This double portrait of Susanne and Ilse, aged three and five respectively, was painted in Germany in 1933 before the family emigrated. It was painted by German artist Joseph Oppenheimer (1876–1966), who was well known for his portraits, landscapes and still life work. He painted the girls with two of their toys, a teddy bear and a toy poodle. The girls are also wearing the two dresses shown below, which along with the portrait were donated to the Museum by the youngest sister, Susanne.

Pedigree Dolls and Toys was part of the internationally significant Lines Bros. toy company founded in 1919. Launched in 1963 as a British version of the teen fashion doll, Sindy competed for popularity with American rival Barbie. Sindy was arguably Pedigree's most successful doll, intended to reflect a more down-to-earth 'girl next door'. Sindy's 1963 launch outfit, pictured first on the left, was known as the 'Weekender', and comprised a stripy jumper and flared trousers. The other three outfits shown in the photograph are from the 1968 ranges. See also p.107

RUBIK'S CUBE
Designed by Ernő Rubik
Europe, 1980s
V&A: Misc.524–1988

The Rubik's Cube was invented in 1977 by an Hungarian sculptor and lecturer on interior design, Ernő Rubik. He sold the toy, originally called the Hungarian Magic Cube, in Budapest toy shops before American company Ideal Toys bought and distributed the puzzle more widely in the 1980s. The Rubik's Cube provided a challenging puzzle that appealed to children and adults. Built around an expertly engineered internal mechanism, the Cube could be turned and twisted in hundreds of different ways on a grid matrix. To complete the puzzle, each face of the Cube must be made up of squares of the same colour.

BABIES &
CHILDCARE

Until the twentieth century, childbirth and infancy were often hazardous times; many children did not survive to adulthood because of illness, the limitations of medicine, bad diet, lack of hygiene and poor living conditions. With developments in research in these areas during the nineteenth century, and increased sophistication of manufactured tools such as feeding apparatus, the life expectancy and ease of care of infants gradually began to improve.

High infant mortality and the uncertainty of a long and healthy life, meant that, for Christians, baptizing a baby soon after its birth was essential. Ceremonies marked other key milestones in a child's development, and were usually accompanied by particular gifts or clothing, such as child-sized gold or silverware christening sets, or a child's first pair of shoes.

The changing size and make-up of the family unit impacted on the way in which a child was reared; babies were not always brought up exclusively by their mothers, for example. In many upper- and middle-class homes, a child would be placed with a wet nurse for feeding, often having limited contact with its parents. For less well-off families, child rearing tended to be a family affair, with the mother and immediate family caring for infants.

There have been many different ideas over time about what is 'best' for a baby. Swaddling an infant – tightly binding them in layers of cloth to restrict movement – was intended to keep the baby warm and secure, and was thought to help the development of straight and strong limbs. This technique was common in Britain until the end of the eighteenth century, but was eventually abandoned in favour of looser clothing, which allowed the child to move, play and be changed more easily.

Furniture designed specifically for children, with the exception of practical pieces such as highchairs, was not widely evident in households until the nineteenth century, when there was an increased appetite for child-related products. This led to an explosion of goods that were designed for babies and children but marketed to parents – some highly practical, others whimsical and entertaining, but all specific to a child's early years.

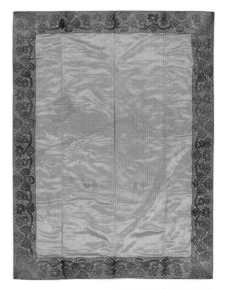

BEARING CLOTH (DETAIL)
England, 17th century
V&A: B.90–2009

CHRISTENING GOWN
England, 1900–20
V&A: Misc.217–1982

Bearing cloths, such as this silk satin and metal thread example, were ceremonial garments, wrapped around a swaddled infant during their baptism. Bearing cloths were a precursor to christening gowns and were usually highly ornate in their decoration. This bearing cloth passed through many generations of the same family since it was made in the seventeenth century, until it was donated to the Museum in 2009.

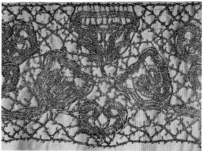

During the seventeenth century, total immersion in water during baptism was common and the bearing cloth would be removed prior to the child being immersed in order to preserve the garment. Christening gowns became popular when this practice became less common, and allowed the infant's clothing, rather than an outer bearing cloth, to be lavishly decorated.

A gown was usually worn by each child in a family and then handed down to the next generation. This simple linen christening gown with lace insertions and pink ribbons has gained the nickname 'The Bin Dress', because it was rescued by the donor's family from a rubbish bin. It is unlikely that we will ever discover the reason it was originally discarded: perhaps there was a dispute or even a tragedy in the family, or maybe it was simply considered too old-fashioned for further use.

This oak highchair, the earliest in the Museum's collection, is thought to date from as early as 1640: the date 1680 and the initials 'R.W' are carved on the back. Made from solid turned oak, it has been ornately carved with scrollwork and inlaid with floral motifs made from holly and bog wood. This chair did not come with a means of fixing the child into place, nor did it have a feeding tray on which to eat. The chair would have been pulled tight to the table and would have relied on the child propping themselves up with the use of the small step. See also pp.13, 34

PORTRAIT OF A BABY
Artist unknown
England, 1690–1730
V&A: B.447-1994

It was unusual in eighteenth-century Britain to paint a portrait of a baby by itself; they were usually part of a family group. Single portraits do exist of babies made after their death, but they would often be depicted in burial clothes. Here the emphasis is on the strong and healthy appearance of the child, who was perhaps the artist's own. See also p.42

SWADDLING BAND
France, 18th century
V&A: B.13-2001

Swaddling, an ancient tradition of clothing and protecting a baby, was practised in Britain up to the end of the eighteenth century, perhaps because of its simplicity, and endured in some countries into the twentieth century. A swaddling band is a single narrow piece of cloth, often made of linen. Several metres long, they restrict the movement of the child with successive tightly bound layers. The top visible layer of this band has been delicately embroidered and would have been used by and made for a wealthy family; commonly, other bands were more plain. Swaddling was intended to keep the baby warm and secure. It was also thought to prevent deformities of posture by keeping the body straight within the tight bindings. This involved the use of additional swaddling garments, in particular the stay band: a strip of fabric that would run down the length of the baby's back and attach to the baby's cap to provide support.

BABY WALKER
England, 1700–50
V&A: W.36–1937

Walking aids for young children have existed in Europe since the Middle Ages. Common designs included a railed panel or enclosed frame on wheels, designed to stabilize the child when learning to walk. The hexagonal enclosed frame walker shown here became increasingly popular at the beginning of the eighteenth century. Debate about the safety of baby walkers and whether they actually help a child to learn to walk is longstanding. Do they promote over-dependence and hinder the natural walking process, or does increased mobility and stability for the child using a walker lead to accidents around the home? Despite these concerns, the basic design of baby walkers is little changed in many of today's models. See also p.28

PUDDING HAT
England, 1775–1800
V&A: B.81–1995

Many small children in the seventeenth and eighteenth centuries wore this type of 'pudding' hat, to protect them from head injuries if they fell while learning to walk. Designed to fasten horizontally around the head above the ears, the 'pudding' consists of a horseshoe-shaped roll of glazed pink cotton with four lightly padded triangular flaps, fastening together over the head. The nickname comes from the padded roll's similarity of shape and size to the type of sausage called 'pudding'. See also p.27

BABY'S CRADLE
Europe, c.1810
V&A: W.5–1936

Cradles have been used for hundreds of years, with surviving examples dating back to the fifteenth century. A separate bed prevented babies being accidentally smothered by a parent and formed a means of providing enclosed warmth and protection. Cradles have commonly offered a soothing rocking motion, particularly when babies were swaddled and did not have the freedom to move to occupy themselves. Early cradles comprised a simple wooden box on rockers, but with no secure mechanism to prevent over-rocking, babies often fell out on to the floor, or worse still, into a nearby fireplace.

This incredibly elaborate cradle has a boat shape typical of French design, and highly ornate applied gilt ormolu motifs more typical of German style; it would have belonged to a very wealthy family. The top of the cradle, from which the drapes hang, originally featured the head of a swan watching proudly over the child to match the gilt swan motifs on the cradle's body. See also p.26

PIN CUSHIONS
United Kingdom, 1830–60
V&A: Misc.142–1985, Misc.238–1988 and
Misc.93–1985

Pin cushions were a popular gift to a new mother, often given as part of a layette. Pins and embroidery were used on these cushions in a decorative way, displaying sweet messages welcoming the baby, similar to those now displayed on 'new arrival' cards. They were particularly popular in the nineteenth century when childhood was celebrated in a newly sentimental light.

Pins were commonly used to fasten clothing, even for a baby's garments. They were expertly handmade and therefore an expensive household item, and it was important to have a place to store them safely. The cushions were stuffed with a heavy substance that could also keep the pins sharp and free from dirt and rust. See also p.43

WEIGHING AND EXERCISE CHAIR
Designed by Edward Emmons
United Kingdom, 1880
V&A: Misc.59–1990

Until the twentieth century specific food requirements for babies and children were not well understood, resulting in bland, overcooked and stodgy food that did not contain enough protein or fibre. This led to concerns that children would suffer from malnutrition and be underweight.

This chair was invented by Edward Emmons in the USA in 1856 and had a later UK patent. The chair's structure could be transformed in shape to utilize two functions: one which would allow the child to play and exercise by rocking and bouncing in the chair; and a spring scale mechanism that would weigh the child to monitor its growth and development.

SILVER RATTLE
Manufactured by Saunders & Shepherd
England, 1901
V&A: Misc.90–1963

Rattles made from a variety of materials have been documented as early as the second century BC, and have been used by children as both plaything and developmental tool. This rattle includes bells and a whistle, the noise of which was intended to occupy the child as well as to ward off evil. Rattles often included an element of coral or bone, such as the bone ring attached to this example. The hard surface of the bone provided an ideal aid for teething.

BREAST PUMP

Manufactured by S. Maw Son & Thompson
England, c.1905
V&A: Misc.470–1985

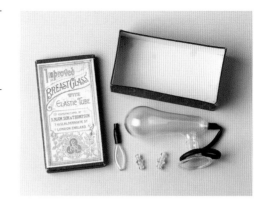

The breast pump dates from 1854, when it was patented by O.H. Needham in the USA. Pumps were used to express milk, which was then fed to a baby via a bottle, allowing a baby to be fed by carers other than the mother. Milk could also be expressed and then stored for additional feeds.

The hand-operated device used a ball pump, suction funnel and relieving chamber, the motion of which would have imitated the sucking motion of an infant. It was not until later in the twentieth century that easier-to-use, mechanized versions were developed. As with feeding bottles, it would have been essential to make sure all parts were easily washable.

FEEDING BOTTLE

Manufactured by Allen and Hanburys Ltd
England, 1911
V&A: Misc.228–1979

Over the centuries, feeding equipment such as bottles for liquids, and pap boats for semi-solid foods, known as pap, were commonly used for infants. These vessels were made from a variety of materials, including pewter, ceramics, silver and, later, glass and plastic. Many of these vessels had intricate shapes, which often had narrow openings for the baby to feed through. This made them difficult to clean adequately, causing a dangerous build-up of bacteria that could have put an infant at risk.

Pharmaceutical company Allen and Hanburys Ltd, founded in 1715, introduced a revolutionary double-ended glass feeder in 1895. The child could feed at one end, drawing an even flow of milk enabled by the pressure valve at the opposite end of the bottle. These mass-manufactured bottles were easy to clean and proved hugely popular. This bottle is probably an example of their updated 1911 model that remained a popular choice for several decades, until its sideways 'banana' shape was replaced with the more familiar upright feeders of today.

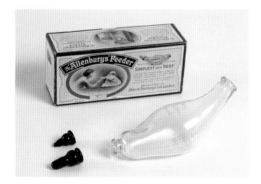

THE CROCKER TWINS
England, 1917
V&A: Misc.451–1991

These photographs of twins Joan and Jack
Crocker were taken on their third birthday.
The first photograph shows the twins in
very similar dresses, which children of both
sexes wore in their early years. The second
photograph shows Joan still in her dress,
but Jack has been 'breeched'; dressed in his
first pair of trousers. Common in Europe for
centuries, the ceremony of breeching, which
usually took place between five and seven
years of age, was an important milestone
in a boy's life. It was often accompanied by
his first haircut and the expectation that he
became more grown up. The practice only
started to wane in the 1920s. See also p.55

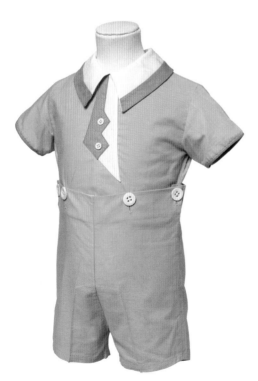

BUSTER SUIT
Europe, 1925–35
V&A: Misc.559–1986

Museum of Childhood

ROYALE PRAM
Manufactured by The Royal Baby
Carriage Co. (A&F Saward)
England, 1959
V&A: Misc.318–1987

Popular from the eighteenth century, miniature carriages pulled by an animal such as a pony, or even by an adult, were a luxury leisure item. As a development of this idea, the perambulator (or pram) was first manufactured during the 1840s and aimed to provide practical transport for children as an alternative to carrying a child. The pram began as an upright chair on three wheels, similar in design to the Bath chair. Although initially popular, this style, without any straps to hold the child in place or brakes to control the vehicle, was not a safe design. Subsequent styles included the mail cart, modelled on a postman's delivery cart, and the bassinet, a cradle on wheels intended for very small babies. These prams had the advantage that the child could lie down comfortably and securely and also face their carer.

The classic deep shape of the Royale pram was popular from around the 1930s until the 1960s. By this stage in the evolution of the pram, the suspension was much smoother and the steering and design of the carriages made them much safer and easier to use. Styles similar to this prevailed for much of the twentieth century until lighter weight, more compact models became available.

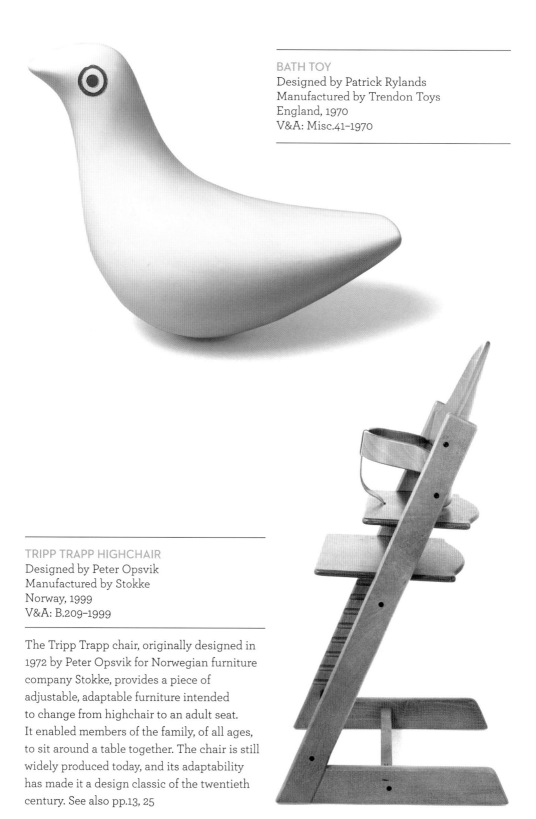

BATH TOY
Designed by Patrick Rylands
Manufactured by Trendon Toys
England, 1970
V&A: Misc.41–1970

TRIPP TRAPP HIGHCHAIR
Designed by Peter Opsvik
Manufactured by Stokke
Norway, 1999
V&A: B.209–1999

The Tripp Trapp chair, originally designed in
1972 by Peter Opsvik for Norwegian furniture
company Stokke, provides a piece of
adjustable, adaptable furniture intended
to change from highchair to an adult seat.
It enabled members of the family, of all ages,
to sit around a table together. The chair is still
widely produced today, and its adaptability
has made it a design classic of the twentieth
century. See also pp.13, 25

UNION JACK NAPPY
Manufactured by Ella's House
Scotland, 2002
V&A: B.8–2003

Diaper is a type of cloth with a lozenge-style pattern that was commonly used to make a nappy. Although disposable absorbent pads were available to insert into nappies from the 1880s, cloth nappies were predominantly used until the 1940s when the convenient and truly disposable nappy was developed. In more recent years, with a growing concern for environmental issues, the reusable, washable nappy has made a comeback.

The nappy shown here is made in fabric printed with the Union Jack design and is lined with a disposable absorbent hemp fleece fabric. It was produced as a souvenir for the Golden Jubilee of Queen Elizabeth II in 2002 by Ella's House, a company that specializes in the use of environmentally friendly materials.

EAMES ELEPHANT
Designed by Charles and Ray Eames
Manufactured by Vitra
Switzerland, 2007 (from original 1945 design)
V&A: B.257–2009

CHILDHOOD & SOCIETY

At different times, childhood has been perceived as a necessary stage from which to graduate into adulthood, where one could be considered 'useful'; it has also been regarded as the 'golden age' of a person's life. It does, however, remain a varied experience, and the concept of 'childhood' is effectively the product of a constantly changing, adult-led society as well as a personal experience.

Prior to the eighteenth century, the Church was central in guiding public opinion and, for many, children were viewed as the product of original sin, in need of reform. Writers and social commentators such as John Locke (1632–1704) and Jean-Jacques Rousseau (1712–78) developed radical concepts concerning work, education, development and play that embodied the idea of childhood as a distinct and significant stage of life. In his book, *Some Thoughts Concerning Education* (1693), Locke referred to the child as a *tabula rasa*, a blank slate, from which they could learn through experience and develop rationally into the adult world. Rousseau's book *Emile* (1762) argued that a child should develop in line with nature and self-discovery and learn through the consequences of their actions. Although these ideas did not immediately filter through society, many social changes for children were eventually influenced by such theories.

Children faced a number of significant issues: poverty, abandonment, homelessness, illness, overwork, and lack of education or care. During the eighteenth and particularly the nineteenth centuries, new reform laws were introduced to tackle these issues. Institutions such as charity schools in the eighteenth century, and similar ragged schools in the nineteenth century – for children whose ragged clothes reflected their destitution and poverty – were also established to protect and help the vulnerable.

The twentieth century brought further cultural and social changes, as well as first-hand experience of war, into the lives of modern British children. The development of a welfare state, a national education system, the idea of the teenager, and the increasing gaze of the media on 'the child' have all played their part in shaping notions of childhood.

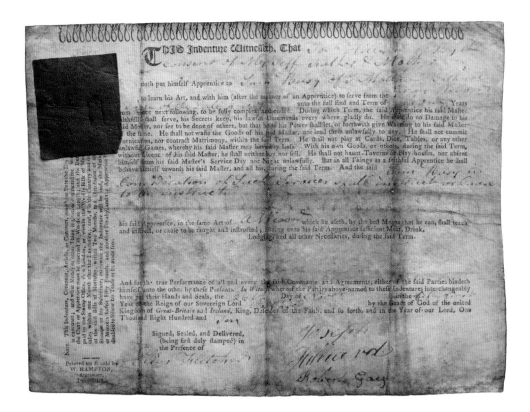

APPRENTICE'S INDENTURE
Printed for and sold by W. Hampton
England, 1810
V&A: Misc.21B–1923

An indenture was a legal document that was signed by an apprentice and his master on agreement of the conditions of an apprenticeship. The master had to provide training in the given trade as well as 'sufficient meat, drink, lodging and all other necessities'. Indentures date back to the Middle Ages, when master craftsmen such as blacksmiths, weavers and tailors would benefit from cheap labour by taking on a child, usually in their early teens, to work for them. Such training would have been a good option for a child and was not an easy opportunity to come by, often having to be bought via a parish council or public charity in the case of the poor. The conditions were often hard for the apprentice. In this case, thirteen-year-old Joseph Hilliard, who was to become a weaver's apprentice, had to promise to 'not commit fornication, nor contract matrimony... not to play cards, dice, tables or any other unlawful games... not haunt taverns or play houses, nor absent himself from his master's service day or night'. By signing the contract he committed to seven years of labour. With the dawn of the Industrial Revolution, apprenticeships to become master craftsmen became less popular and children found greater opportunities for work in factories. See also p.47

LOCHGELLY TAWSE
Produced by John J. Dick
Scotland, 1972
V&A: B.100–1996

POSTURE BOARD
England, c.1820
V&A: B.1–2009

DEPORTMENT CHAIR
England, c.1835
V&A: W.80–1929

Discipline of children at home and school
has involved various forms of physical
correction. Corporal punishment was
practised in British state schools as recently
as the 1980s, until it was banned under a
clause of the Education Act of 1986. It was
still in use in some public schools until its
complete ban in 1998. Several devices were
used to inflict punishment, such as a cane
or whip; in Scotland the most common tool
for punishment was the tawse, a thick, heavy
strap of leather split into sections at the end,
with which to hit a child's hands.

A form of non-violent discipline was
concerned with correcting posture. Between
the 1780s and the 1850s, middle- and upper-
class girls were often subject to the posture
or deportment board. The board, positioned
behind the back of the girl and held in place
by her arms, pulled the shoulders back and
produced an upright stance. This board
has been inscribed with the names of five
children who are thought to have used it:
Sally, Gatie, Tiny, Ada and Maud.

Deportment chairs had a similar purpose.
Their straight back, tall legs and small cane
seat were intended to make children sit up
straight. It would have been difficult and
uncomfortable to sit on the chair for any
length of time. See also p.96

THE MATHS LESSON
Artist unknown
England, 1840–50
V&A: B.2–2007

See also p.15

EDUCATIONAL SAMPLE BOX
England, c.1850
V&A: B.5–2009

Specimen boxes were a popular method
of experimental education for privileged
children in the nineteenth century. Based
on the early ideas of educationalist Johann
Heinrich Pestalozzi (1746–1827), children
were encouraged to learn organically and
creatively, exploring to find an answer
to problems, instead of learning through
repetition. Pestalozzi believed that children
learned best using a combination of head,
heart and hand, and that their education
should include practical methodology as well
as ideologies of freedom and social justice.
The box has several layers of fascinating
specimens for a child to examine, including
mercury, geological samples and feathers.
See also p.50

Museum of Childhood

SAMPLER BOOK

By Ellen Mahon
Ireland, 1852–4
V&A: T.123–1958

Girls and boys were generally raised to adhere to different social expectations and thus their education often differed. Boys from wealthy families would usually be sent to school, while girls tended to be educated at home, preparing them to care for their husband and family, or for their employment as a domestic servant. Some would have been apprenticed in skills such as embroidery.

Sampler books have been used as a means of education for girls for hundreds of years, and comprise a series of techniques that a girl must master. This book features a complete education in embroidery and dressmaking, including pattern-cut pieces for miniature clothing, patchwork and quilting, and the all-important and beautifully executed darning stitch.

Childhood & Society

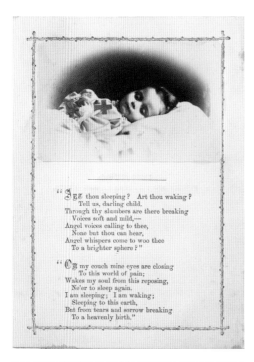

MEMENTO MORI
Printed and published by John Hodges
United Kingdom, 1850–1900
V&A: B.85–1995

**CARTE-DE-VISITE OF THE DECEASED
ALFRED OWENS, AGED 10 MONTHS**
United Kingdom, 1868
V&A: B.84–1995

Throughout the nineteenth century, child mortality was high, particularly as a result of now-treatable illnesses such as measles and tuberculosis, or as a consequence of hazardous working conditions for older children. Mourning for the dead was a common part of life, and memorial cards were circulated to friends and family. With the invention of photography in the nineteenth century, these cards often included a photograph of the deceased child. Although the idea of recording a dead child laid to rest may seem morbid now, it was common to represent the dead child as if they were sleeping peacefully, rather than to reproduce a memorial image of the child when they were alive. See also pp.16, 26

PIN CUSHION DOLL DRESSED AS A LONDON CHARITY SCHOOLGIRL
England, 1860s
V&A: T.104–1935

This doll is dressed in the typical uniform of a charity school pupil of the nineteenth century. By this point charity schools were well established in Britain, many of them having been set up in the eighteenth century. They were usually run by local parishes and supported by subscriptions and appeals. They took in children whose parents could not afford to look after them, often providing free clothing, shelter and a basic education in reading, writing and religious teachings. Although the aims of charity schools were intended to be positive, and some children were found apprenticeships or in rarer cases even sent on to university, many of the schools were, in reality, hard and sometimes unsanitary places for children to grow up in. See also pp.29, 44

ONLY A HALFPENNY
Painted by A. Burgess
England, 1868
V&A: 1210–1886

Children living in poverty and the prevalence of street children were significant problems when this picture was painted. Through the implementation of the New Poor Law of 1834, many destitute children and their families were removed from the streets or their homes to live and labour in a workhouse. Although this image shows children begging, it presents a sentimental view: the girls are pretty and well fed and, although in tattered clothing, the general feel of the image is of a staged scene rather than an accurate depiction of the harsher realities of life of the poor or destitute.

POSTCARDS
Printed and published at the press
of Dr Barnardo's Homes
England, c.1900
V&A: B.184 & 185–1993

Until the first Education Act of 1870, there
was no national education system in place.
Dr Thomas Barnardo began his charitable
work with children in 1867 by founding a
ragged school in East London, which poor
children could attend for a basic education at
no cost. In 1870, Barnardo went on to set up
a home for destitute boys in Stepney, after
a pupil, Jim Jarvis, showed him children
sleeping rough in the area. When a boy who
had been turned away because the home
was full was found dead of starvation and
exposure, the motto 'No Destitute Child
Ever Refused Admission' was adopted,
and Barnardo redoubled his efforts to help
the poorest and most vulnerable children
by establishing similar homes across the
UK. These postcards, printed over 30
years after the founding of his first school,
show disadvantaged children being given
purposeful employment. See also p.43

MUTTON BONE DOLL
England, 1890–1920
V&A: Misc.12–1924

Edward Lovett (1852–1933) worked in a
London bank, but he was passionately
interested in the origin and meaning of toys.
He collected and made toys from a variety
of natural materials. His collections finally
took over his house, so much so that his
wife eventually left him. This doll, part of
the collection he donated to the Museum in
1924, is made from an old mutton bone. The
doll was bought by Lovett from a child on
the street in Bethnal Green. The child has
given the bone some crudely painted facial
features and sewn fabric scraps together to
act as a dress and bonnet. At the beginning
of the twentieth century, Bethnal Green
was an extremely poor part of London, and
children living there may have made their
own toys out of things they found lying
around. See also pp.18, 92, 97, 102

Museum of Childhood

ROYAL HORSE ARTILLERY GUN
Manufactured by Britains Ltd
England, c.1900
V&A: B.118–2009

War and conflict have always been a part
of active play, reflecting the age in which
the toys were made. This has resulted
in a wide range of toys and games, from
seventeenth-century miniature toy pewter
muskets available from street sellers, to toy
versions of real guns, to the hyper-realistic
and sophisticated combat computer games
of modern times. During the nineteenth and
twentieth centuries, miniature and accurate
armies of toy soldiers could be bought from
Britains Ltd. More recently, representation of
violent conflict through these types of toys
has come under increasing scrutiny, and
the question of whether such toys provoke
violence in children is one still asked today.
See also pp.99, 109

SCHOOLGIRLS IN A CLASSROOM
Photographed by J. & G. Taylor
England, 1910–19
V&A: Misc.1056–1992

LABOUR CERTIFICATE
Produced for Leeds Education Authority
England, 1914
V&A: B.21–1995

In 1914, Annie Waggonheim was 13 years old, the age at which it was then permitted to leave school and begin work. With successive education acts, this rose to 14 years old in 1918, 15 in 1944, and 16 in 1972. These changes were often strongly opposed at the time by employers and parents, and also by pupils themselves. Labour certificates were introduced via the Employment of Children Act 1903 to prove a competent level of education had been attained in order to enter the workforce. Unfortunately, this put

pressure on bright children from poorer families to leave school as soon as possible in order to bring in an extra wage.

The 1903 Act also limited the hours and times a child could be employed for, and outlawed many of the bad practices relating to the employment of children. The Act was hard to enforce, however, particularly in remote villages, or large cities with a high proportion of migrant labourers. See also p.38

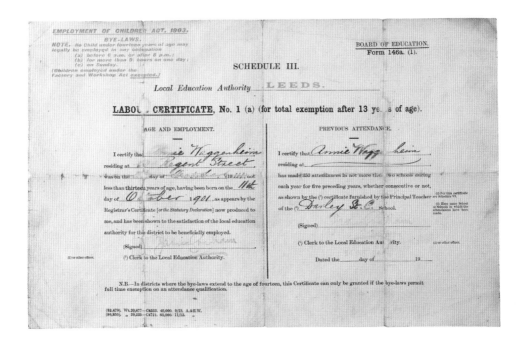

WOLF CUB ENROLMENT CERTIFICATE
Designed by C.S. Chapman
United Kingdom, 1923
V&A: B.34–1993

BOY SCOUT'S UNIFORM
Manufactured for The Scout Association
United Kingdom, post-1967
V&A: B.421–1994

Many organized youth movements originated at the beginning of the twentieth century, and aimed to involve children in meaningful group activity and equip them with the skills and socialization required for adult life. This might include specific moral, religious, spiritual or political learning. Robert Baden-Powell (1857–1941) founded the Boy Scouts in 1907, and its junior counterpart, the Cub Scouts, in 1916.

Many youth movements, including the Scouts and Cubs, formed their own identity through the wearing of uniforms and badges and through ceremonies, songs and rules. Baden-Powell's groups had an emphasis on religion and were run with near-military precision; the original *Scouting for Boys* handbook, published in 1908, was based on military principles.

Museum of Childhood

TEDDY BEAR WITH GAS MASK
Manufactured by Steiff
Germany, c.1910
V&A: Misc.787–1992

EVACUATION NOTICE,
ST PATRICK'S SCHOOL, WAPPING
England, 1939
V&A: B.19–1995

During the Second World War, all UK civilians were issued with gas masks for fear of air raids employing poisonous gas. Ted's outfit includes a homemade gas mask, made to encourage his owner Elizabeth to get used to wearing a gas mask herself.

From 1939, many children were evacuated from major cities away from the danger of bombing to safer 'reception' areas in the countryside. The scheme had mixed results. Many hosts and guests found it difficult to settle down together, at least to begin with.

Some children had good living conditions and caring hosts, while others were abused and neglected, often suffering in silence for years afterwards. Some evacuee children returned home in preference to staying away from their families, and some parents refused to send their children away at all. See also pp.19, 100, 111

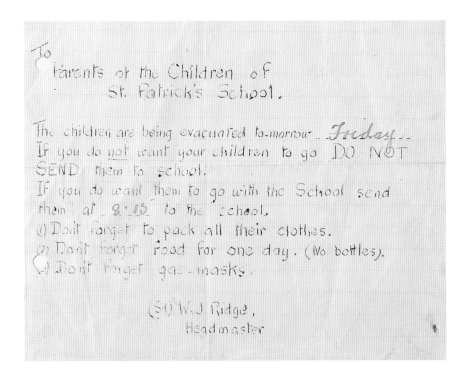

To
Parents of the Children of
St. Patrick's School.

The children are being evacuated to-morrow _Friday_.
If you do not want your children to go DO NOT
SEND them to school.
If you do want them to go with the School send
them at 8.15 to the school.
(1) Don't forget to pack all their clothes.
(2) Don't forget food for one day. (No bottles).
(3) Don't forget gas-masks.

(Sd) W. J. Ridge,
Headmaster

GIFT NO.5
Designed by Friedrich Froebel
Japan, 1980s
V&A: Misc.1095–1992

Friedrich Froebel (1782–1852) was one of the most influential educationalists in history. He studied under Johann Heinrich Pestalozzi, and believed that children had great capabilities for learning using play. He became a teacher and designed a series of educational processes known as Occupations, comprising activities to develop skills such as carving, weaving and drawing, and learning toys called Gifts (*Fröbelgaben*). Children were expected to work through the series of Gifts, and as their knowledge became more sophisticated, the complexities and number of shapes in the Gifts increased. This Gift, number 5, was the last one to be produced in Froebel's lifetime and contains many simple wooden geometric shapes that fit into a wooden cube.

The Gifts originally designed by Froebel in the 1830s have been frequently reproduced, as with this set made in Japan, and are still used as teaching aids. See also p.40

MONTESSORI DRESSING FRAME
Designed by Maria Montessori
Europe, 1987
V&A: Misc.3–1988

Maria Montessori (1870–1952) was the first woman to qualify as a doctor in Italy, where she was born. She spent the early part of her career studying education and behavioural and mental disorders in children. She began to observe and successfully teach children who were considered mentally 'defective'. This fused her knowledge of medicine with education and went on to inform her life's work. In 1906 her expertise was utilized in the development of the first of many Casa Dei Bambini, or children's houses, and she spent her career involved with schools and education. In 1909 her book *Scientific Pedagogy as Applied to Child Education in the Children's Houses* was published. This book was later renamed *The Discovery of the Child,* and its principles and teaching methods are still in use today.

Montessori argued that there were 'universal characteristics of childhood', regardless of the child, and that all children wanted to learn and to be independent. She was the first educator to develop child-size furniture and equipment, such as this frame apparatus. The frame uses simple methods to teach a child how to dress, as well as helping their coordination and motor skills.

Museum of Childhood

TEENAGE PARENTS
Photographed by John Heywood
United Kingdom, 1989
V&A: Misc.1087–1992

There have always been young parents, but the age at which one is acknowledged to pass from childhood to adulthood has changed over time, and the social construct of the 'teenager' is a twentieth-century phenomenon. The proud teenage parents pose outside their home with their young baby. In the modern world children are effectively viewed as minors for longer than ever before, yet at the same time they are exposed to a world of adult behaviours at even younger ages. See also pp.70, 88

IDENTITY & CLOTHING

Over the last 300 years, changing attitudes towards childhood have been reflected in the development of children's clothing. Wearing clothes for 'best' might appear outdated now, when casual styles prevail, but it was the norm in past generations. It is these 'best' clothes, rather than those of a normal and everyday function, that tend to survive in greater numbers in museums.

It is a common misconception that children were always dressed as miniature adults in the past. There have been periods in history where adults' and children's styles were more aligned, perhaps most apparent in the formal wear of the eighteenth century. Equally, there have been times when garments marked childhood out as a separate stage in life. Leading strings – long bands of material attached to the back of a dress – were a restrictive aid similar to modern reins, common for a child's earlier years and worn symbolically by older girls, but not found on adult garments.

Clothing can give children a particular identity. Some garments define age, gender or class, others are worn for a specific purpose, such as school uniform, practical work garments, mourning clothes or Sunday best. They can also reflect times of social upheaval or reform. The liberty bodice was an undergarment produced from 1908, the result of dress reform that began in the late nineteenth century; it was a softer and less restrictive alternative to its predecessor, the corset.

In some cases children's dress actually led adult fashion: in the 1800s it was girls who first wore high-waisted dresses made from light and loose fabrics; in the 1920s they led the way with waistlines dropped to below the hip; and in the 1960s women mimicked the young shapes and styles of girls' dresses.

Clothing can also mark symbolic milestones in a child's development: a christening gown, a girl's first bra, or a boy's transition from dress to trousers. The 1950s saw the birth of the teenager, resulting in styles and trends specifically for young people in the awkward years before adulthood, and an explosion of different youth cultures that could be signalled via clothing. Now, children of an increasingly young age are able to express their identity through their clothing, and wearing the 'right' clothes or labels has become an increasing pressure.

CHILD'S WARDROBE
Built by Edmund Joy
England, 1712
V&A: W.36–1930

PORTRAIT OF A YOUNG GIRL
Artist unknown
United Kingdom, c.1730
V&A: Misc.199–1990

This painting shows the formal clothes typical in the eighteenth century for young girls and women alike. Unlike a woman's gown, this girl's bodice was laced at the back and she would therefore require some form of assistance in order to dress. The stiffened and tightly laced bodice formed a small, restrictive waistline which, coupled with a full skirt, accentuated the waist-to-hip ratio thought to be attractive in this period. Dresses such as the one in this portrait were typically made of silk for older girls; younger girls wore cotton or linen. See also p.14

BOY'S ROBE
France, *c.*1750
V&A: T.362–1920

BOY'S RED DRESS
England, *c.*1850
V&A: T.83–1966

Dresses for young boys were common until the 1920s, although styles of dress changed over time. Boys wore dresses, tunics or robes into early childhood, usually until the age of five to seven. The origin of the custom is not known, although it may be simply that before about 1550, both sexes and all ages wore tunics and gowns of some sort, and young children's fashions are often slow to change. In practical terms it would also have been easier to change nappies if the child wore skirts rather than trousers.

By the Victorian period, boys' dresses, such as this example of red wool with black velvet trim, were often distinguished from those of girls through the use of bolder colours and details made from fabrics such as leather or velvet. See also p.32

BOY'S STRIPED SUIT
England, c.1760
V&A: T.113–1953

See also p.57

EMBROIDERED MUSLIN GOWN
England, 1812–15
V&A: T.29–1936

From the 1770s onward, there was a
change in the shape and material used
for children's clothes, which reflected
romantic attitudes of freedom for children,
later influenced by the French Revolution
and popularized by figures such as Jean-
Jacques Rousseau. Lighter materials, such
as cotton muslins, and less restrictive
shapes were introduced, which freed girls
from the restraining corsetry and tiny
waistlines of previous styles.

The ornate tambour work embroidery on this
very fine muslin fabric – probably imported
from India – and trained skirt would not have
been practical for everyday wear, and would
suggest this dress was owned by a girl from a
wealthy family and probably saved for 'best'.
See also p.14

BOY'S SUIT WITH GREEN JACKET
Scotland, 1825–30
V&A: T.144–1962

This suit is a later version of the close-fitting skeleton suit, comprising high-waisted trousers buttoned onto a jacket, in this case to the underlying waistcoat, to create an all-in-one costume. This style of suit became popular in the 1790s and was worn specifically by young boys. They were intended to be a new and comfortable style of garment that allowed ease of movement. Charles Dickens describes his own experience of wearing one a little differently:

...one of those straight blue cloth cases in which small boys used to be confined, before belts and tunics had come in, and old notions had gone out: an ingenious contrivance for displaying the full symmetry of a boy's figure, by fastening him into a very tight jacket, with an ornamental row of buttons over each shoulder, and then buttoning his trousers over it, so as to give his legs the appearance of being hooked on, just under the armpit.

Sketches by Boz, Charles Dickens (1836)
See also pp.32, 56

GIRL'S DRESS
England, 1850s
V&A: T.403–1971

The girl who wore this dress was probably
around six years old. It is typical of mid-
nineteenth-century dress styles for both
women and girls, with a tightly fitting waist
and a flared skirt. The dress is made of blue
shot silk and has a striking Greek key pattern
in black velvet ribbon on the sleeves and
skirt hem. For young girls, dresses were worn
to the knee, supported by stiffened layers of
petticoats and with decorative drawers as a
feature at the bottom of the dress.

Museum of Childhood

CHILD'S SHOES
Manufactured by C.S. Gilman
England, *c.*1851
V&A: T.276–1963

See also p.69

CRINOLINE
United Kingdom, 1860s
V&A: B.18–2002

Cage crinolines gave support and shape to skirts without the need for the large number of petticoats that had been previously worn. They helped rid girls of over-complicated, heavy and hot layers, however they were by no means an unrestrictive form of dress. This crinoline is probably for an older girl because it reaches to the ankle; younger girls would have worn short skirts with a short crinoline underneath.

From the 1860s, the weight and volume of skirts gradually pushed to the rear, developing into bustles in the 1880s. With the placement of fabric and bows and perhaps a small padded attachment underneath, young girls could simulate more structural adult versions of the bustle. See also pp.62, 63

Identity & Clothing

SMOCK
England, 1860s
V&A: Misc.96–1982

GIRL'S DRESS
Designed by Liberty & Co.
England, 1930s
V&A: B.300–1996

Working adults and children in rural areas generally wore very practical clothes, such as smocks. A large amount of hardwearing material was drawn together and gathered by stitches at the front to allow for ease of movement when working. Smocking was also developed into a useful and practical style for children's clothing, as it allowed space for a growing and active body.

From its practical origins, smocking became a largely decorative technique, commonly used in children's fashion garments. The chest and back of this 1930s Liberty print dress are smocked using stem, cable, diamond and wave stitches.

SCOTCH SUIT
Scotland, 1870
V&A: Misc.351–1979

Scotch suits were commercially made versions of Highland dress and included a number of garments such as a kilt, waistcoat, sporran and cap. Scotch suits were among a selection of fanciful outfits for boys, such as the Fauntleroy and sailor suits that became popular in the mid-nineteenth century. They were popularized by Queen Victoria, who liked to dress her sons in them when they resided in Scotland and for formal occasions, such as the opening of the Great Exhibition in 1851. Scotch suits remained popular into the twentieth century, but after the 1920s they tended only to be worn as pageboy outfits for weddings.

ARTS AND CRAFTS CHILD'S COAT
United Kingdom, 1880–95
V&A: B.17–1998

GIRL'S MOURNING COAT
England, *c.*1882
V&A: B.177–2000

This tiny silk coat was made for two-year-old Isabella Ewens on the occasion of her grandmother's funeral in 1882. The shape of the coat, with its 'princess line' – long shaped panels of fabric without a waist seam – finished with Van Dyked tabs along the bottom is typical of girls' styles from the 1880s.

The Victorian tradition of wearing black to mark the death of a relative or even a public figure came with strict protocol that even children were expected to follow, although very young children often wore white when in mourning. There were also particular periods of mourning: full mourning required black garments to be worn; at half mourning, grey and purple colours could be added acceptably to clothing, followed by a gradual return to normal attire, marking the end of the grieving period. See also pp.59, 63

Museum of Childhood

FASHION PLATE FROM THE JOURNAL DES DEMOISELLES ET PETIT COURIER DES DAMES RÉUNIS
France, 1884–90
V&A: E.1283–1959

See also pp.59, 62

BERTIE STONE IN A NORFOLK JACKET AND HAROLD STONE IN A FAUNTLEROY SUIT
Photographed by W.H. Palmer
England, c.1895
V&A: MOC

During the nineteenth century the number of different clothing styles available for boys increased greatly, with boys often having a greater choice for their wardrobes than girls.

The Norfolk jacket was a popular hardwearing structured garment for men. It was typically made of tweed and worn for hunting or other country pursuits. Norfolk jackets for boys were also popular but are a rare find today.

The Fauntleroy suit was first worn around 1860, and was popularized through the illustrations in Frances Hodgson Burnett's *Little Lord Fauntleroy* (1886). This costume was seen as fanciful and theatrical and not for everyday wear, and is often seen in studio portraits from the period. The style references fashions from the seventeenth century, particularly in the distinctive lace collar with breeches and jacket made of velvet.

THE ROYAL NAVY OF ENGLAND & THE STORY OF THE SAILOR SUIT
Published by William Rowe & Co.
Illustrated by Septimus E. Scott
England, c.1895
V&A: B.143–1995

Britain's importance as an influential sea-faring nation during the nineteenth century was reflected in the range of naval attire available for children. The sailor suit was popularized by Queen Victoria, who dressed her son Prince Albert Edward in a specially ordered suit and then commissioned a portrait of him in 1846 by the artist Franz Xavier Winterhalter (1805–73).

Rowe's of Gosport were a leading maker of naval clothing, offering direct copies of regulation Royal Navy garments in adult and child sizes as leisurewear in the 1890s. The popularity of naval-influenced clothing, such as blue-and-white-striped garments and sailor collars, continues today.

GILBERT CATTLEY
England, c.1902
V&A: B.779–1993

This photograph shows Gilbert Cattley in an Eton suit. Such suits began as school uniform for boys who attended the prestigious Eton College, founded in 1440. Aspects of this uniform, particularly the Eton collar, then filtered down to other schools and into formal dress for boys in the nineteenth century.

The Eton collar was deep and stiffened and was attached to the top of a shirt. It would probably have been quite uncomfortable to wear, yet it conveyed a sense of formality and discipline that were seen as beneficial, particularly in a school environment.
See also p.19

CHILDREN ON THE BEACH
Photographed by A.H. Remington
English, 1920–39
V&A: B.277–2010

GYMBO CATALOGUE
Published by Ashworths Ltd
Printed by Shephard & Markham Ltd
England, 1925–30
V&A: B.393–1997

The gymslip was first worn by girls for physical education from the late nineteenth century, and was a part of dress reform that freed girls from the wearing of restrictive clothing. It comprised a loose-fitting, mid-length sleeveless dress usually worn over a short-sleeved blouse and fastened with a belt at the waist. Underneath, girls would usually have worn a Liberty bodice and navy knickers. The loose design of the dress, which was not in itself fitted around the waist, was intended to provide the freedom of movement required for physical exercise. Due to its practicality and comfort, the gymslip was later adopted as a common part of girls' school uniform. See also pp.68, 69

THE LORD MAYOR'S FANCY DRESS BALL
Photographed by Studio of Bassano
England, 1936
V&A: B.22–1996

Fancy dress became very fashionable for adults and children from the 1840s. These portraits, taken at the annual Lord Mayor of London's Fancy Dress Ball, come from a 36-page album of photographs from the studio of famous society photographer Alexander Bassano (1829–1913). They give a great overview of popular themed outfits from the period, and include historical characters, national costumes and conceptual outfits as well as popular favourites Pierrot and fairies. Many costumes of the time could be purchased either ready-made or in pattern form from magazines, or were made from scratch at home.

GIRL'S LIBERTY BODICE
Manufactured by Kosybak
England, 1942–52
V&A: Misc.587–1985

Ideas about dress shapes and layers changed radically at the beginning of the twentieth century, and women and girls in particular were freed from the restrictive corsets or stays of the nineteenth century. The soft but structured Liberty bodice that replaced them allowed a much greater degree of movement and comfort, and was worn by girls as an undergarment into the 1950s. The Liberty bodice shown here was made under the wartime Utility Scheme, where clothing was produced using simple and standard materials and economic cuts of fabric; its distinctive CC41 label is visible at the neck. See also p.67

HEART MOTIF DRESS
Designed by Pierre Cardin for
Neiman Marcus
USA, 1970s
V&A: B.92–2009

Designer labels have become increasingly important to the identity of some children, whether viewed by themselves, their peers, or as a reflection of their parents' taste. Designers normally associated with high-end women's and men's wear are now creating children's ranges in increasing numbers. Pierre Cardin's heart-motif dress was made for the US department store Neiman Marcus in the 1970s. The use of a strong geometric cut and simple colour palate of cream with a red stylized heart motif and border make this a recognizably Cardin-designed dress. See also p.71

Museum of Childhood

THELMA
Drawing by Fyffe Christie
England, 1973
V&A: B.113–2010

School uniforms have given children an enforced identity, linking pupils with each other and their institution. They are generally considered to be a social leveller between children from different backgrounds, but whether to have a uniform is still the cause of much debate. In recent decades, fewer schools have a strict uniform and in many cases it has changed into a more informal style, such as wearing sweatshirts.

Uniformity of dress invites subversion and adaptation by children, particularly by teenagers, who often seek to customize their uniform or wear it incorrectly. Thelma, a student at Barking Abbey School in the 1970s, is depicted here by artist and teacher Fyffe Christie, who spent a decade observing the behaviour and body language of his teenage pupils, quickly sketching them out between lessons. This study captures a sense of the awkward teenager, reflected through body language and a relaxed approach to her uniform. See also p.67

PLIMSOLLS
Designed by Curiosity Shop
Korea, 1975–85
V&A: B.366–1993

See also p.59

Identity & Clothing

SNORKEL PARKA
United Kingdom, 1976
V&A: Misc.588–1992

The parka jacket was originally developed in the late 1940s for US military use and was prized for its practical, hardwearing properties. In civilian wear, parkas became hugely popular, particularly for schoolboys in the 1970s, and were seen as symbols of both Mod and Indie subcultures. They are now considered vintage collectibles, both for their practical attributes and their enduring style appeal.

ON THE WAY TO SCHOOL
Photographed by John Heywood
United Kingdom, 1982
V&A: Misc.1086–1992

Since the 1940s and 1950s, children – and teenagers in particular – have sought a common identity through establishing peer groups and subcultures. An important part of this is reflected through wearing the appropriate clothing or 'uniform', or through rebellious behaviour such as the boys in bomber jackets smoking at the back of the bus. See also pp.51, 88

DRESSING GOWN
Designed by Ladybird
England, 1980s
V&A: Misc.143–1982

Ladybird is one of the most recognizable high-street childrenswear brands of the twentieth century, known for its quality and affordability. Its pyjamas and this iconic dressing gown with ladybird buttons were some of its most successful garments.

Ladybird was started by the Pasold family in Germany in the 1930s, before moving production to the UK during the Second World War. It supplied childrenswear to outlets such as Marks & Spencer and Woolworth's, becoming a brand leader in the 1950s. Initially, a white bear logo was tested for the brand, but was found not to appeal to British buyers; the ladybird was then chosen as a popular alternative, and was particularly successful due to a marketing strategy that placed comic strips featuring cartoon ladybirds in children's publications.

TRAPEZE DRESS
Designed by Phillip Lim
USA, 2007
V&A: B.184–2009

Designer clothing for children is now a big industry, and Phillip Lim's spotty trapeze dress comes from one of his first children's collections. It distills the key design, shape and detailing from his 3.1 women's range down to a child's proportions, enabling a mother and daughter to co-ordinate their styles. See also p.68

Identity & Clothing

LEARNING & DEVELOPMENT THROUGH PLAY

Play can take many forms, and may not even involve manufactured or crafted playthings: a child's imagination is usually sufficient to invent games, friends and fantasy worlds. Outdoor play and sports can help to develop dexterity, a sense of social interaction and a healthy level of competition, although in more recent years, children tend to play outdoors unsupervised less often. From the nineteenth century, the popularity of indoor parlour games and playthings such as optical toys and toy theatres made play an increasingly significant element in family life.

All toys or games can be seen as educational in some way because they engage a child physically, emotionally or mentally. Many have been designed with education as their specific purpose, be it giving moral guidance through board games, teaching history or geography through puzzles, religion through a Noah's ark, or household duties through domestic-themed toys. During the eighteenth and nineteenth centuries, these types of toys would have been a significant part of a child's home education, particularly at a time when there remained emphasis in many Christian movements on correcting sinful behaviour. Educational toys were intended to give children a set of values, skills and knowledge to prepare them for their expected position in the adult world.

So-called traditional toys were popularly produced in Germany from the seventeenth century, and often employed simple wooden shapes, such as building blocks, bricks or carved figures. They were used for the early development of a child's spatial awareness and dexterity, through to more sophisticated modes of play. These types of toys and their educational ethos, celebrated by reformers such as John Locke, Maria Montessori and Friedrich Froebel, have endured in the twentieth century through toymakers such as Paul and Marjorie Abbatt, Kiddicraft and Galt. Their common belief was that simple, well-designed toys appropriate for a child's age, were the key to providing the child with essential developmental skills in or out of the classroom. These toys often combined their learning ethos with simple but pleasing aesthetic qualities that have, in some instances, changed little over time.

THE NUREMBERG HOUSE
Germany, 1673
V&A: W.41–1922

The Nuremberg House is the earliest example in the Museum's significant collection of dolls' houses, dating from 1673. The oldest surviving dolls' houses originating from seventeenth-century Nuremberg would have been specially commissioned and produced by a range of highly skilled craftsmen. They were intended as status symbols for the wealthy, often reflecting a family's position or occupation. This house includes a miniature model of a unicorn mounted on the inside of the house by the front door. In real houses of this period, the unicorn symbol was commonly used to indicate that a house was owned by an apothecary or a chemist.

Dolls' houses were also used as didactic aids to help teach girls their expected domestic duties and household management skills. Various books were available to help with domestic instruction, but with few girls of the time able to read, using dolls' houses as teaching aids proved a popular alternative. It was only from the nineteenth century that dolls' houses became specifically a child's plaything. See also pp.2, 17, 93

Museum of Childhood

LADY CHARLOTTE FINCH'S PUZZLE CABINET
England, c.1750
V&A: B.1–2011

This mahogany cabinet dates from around the mid-1700s and was built to house a collection of 16 dissected maps. These maps, early precursors to the jigsaw puzzle, include some of the earliest known to exist and were originally owned and played with by the children of King George III and Queen Charlotte. It is thought the puzzles were the idea of their governess Lady Charlotte Finch, and would have been kept at the main royal residence at Kew Palace. Some of the puzzles were designed by Charlotte Finch herself, some were drawn by the royal children,

and some were early puzzles made by John Spilsbury, thought to be the first commercial producer of dissected puzzles from around 1760.

A note pinned inside the cabinet records its royal provenance and claims that Lady Charlotte Finch was 'the inventor of dissecting maps... always used in teaching Geography to George the fourth, his Brothers and sisters'; George IV and future monarchs went on to command parts of the globe they had learnt about as children.

'THE JUBILEE' BOARD GAME
Published by John Harris
England, 1810
V&A: E.216–1944

Many historically themed board games produced in Britain tended to focus primarily on British historical events and figures. The Jubilee game is a continuation of Historical Pastime, also published by John Harris, which charted English history from the Norman Conquest to the accession of George III. It is a race game, split into 150 different playing spaces that form a coil. It culminates in King George III's Jubilee at the centre of the board, celebrating his 50 years as monarch. Each square highlights a significant event within his reign, including important scientific and geographic discoveries, as well as more disagreeable events such as riots in London and rebellions in Ireland. See also pp.78, 79, 81, 103, 109

JUVENILE THEATRE
Published by Matthias Trentsensky
Austria, c.1825–80
V&A: E.3856–1953

At the beginning of the nineteenth century, publishers such as Matthias Trentsensky in Austria and William West in England made complete toy theatres, as well as printed paper sheets with characters, prosceniums and scripts. This theatre comes with several of Trentsensky sheets, as well as handmade ones by the children who owned it, and includes scenery depicting Ancient Egypt and a magical fairyland. See also p.83

NOAH'S ARK
Germany, c.1825
V&A: Misc.2–1956

The first known toy arks were handmade by specialist craftsmen in the Oberammergau and Tyrol regions of Germany from the late sixteenth century, and exported to Britain and the colonies. Traditionally the animals were handcarved wooden pieces, later made using tools such as a lathe. The simplicity of their production and design has changed little over the last 300 years.

Arks were considered by many Christian groups to be the only acceptable toy for a child to play with on Sundays, often permitted in between a morning church service and afternoon Sunday school. They taught children the Old Testament story of Noah, but also had a wider educational appeal as they enabled children to learn about the different animals; children in Europe would not have been familiar with creatures such as lions and elephants.

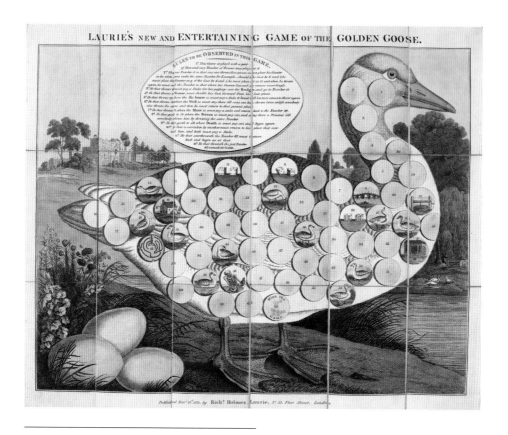

LAURIE'S NEW AND ENTERTAINING GAME
OF THE GOLDEN GOOSE
Published by R.H. Laurie
England, 1831
V&A: Circ.230–1964

The Game of the Golden Goose is generally regarded as the prototype of modern race games. It was devised in Florence, Italy, in the last quarter of the sixteenth century and first came to England in 1597.

A race game usually involves players getting from a start to a finish line, moving round playing squares by using dice or similar devices. In the Game of the Golden Goose, landing on different playing squares provided a moral consequence or a reward; some squares, such as landing on a goose, allowed you to advance, while others required you to move back several places.

Treacherous squares that would hinder your advancement and were to be avoided included going to prison, drinking in an ale house, or even dicing with death. The winner was the first player to land cleanly on the final square, number 63.

The game's popularity continued and it was produced in many different formats. This English version of the game, made in 1831, features the playing squares within the outline image of a goose; the rules are printed on the playing sheet, contained playfully within the shape of an egg. See also pp.76, 79, 81, 103, 109

THE COTTAGE OF CONTENT, OR
RIGHT ROAD AND WRONG WAYS
Published by William Spooner
England, 1848
V&A: E.1785–1954

The Cottage of Content was designed to enable players to choose the correct path in life, through the moral guidance of the game itself. The board is printed with many paths, roads and sites, including Laughing Stock Lane and Bad Boy's Road, and the aim is to reach the Cottage of Content at the top. Severe penalties were meted out if players strayed from the path of goodness and virtue. Both good and bad qualities were displayed in the game to allow the players to understand the difference between right and wrong. As well as being of a moral nature, the game was also intended to be amusing and entertaining. See also pp.76, 78, 81, 103, 109

ZOETROPE
Manufactured by Milton Bradley & Co.
USA, 1880–90
V&A: Misc.76–1963

The word zoetrope is from the Greek *zoe*, meaning life, and *tropos*, meaning turn, and can be interpreted as 'the wheel of life'. The zoetrope was invented by William Horner in 1834 as a form of optical toy and became popular as educational fun for adults. The zoetrope used still images of a developing sequential set, drawn or printed on long strips of paper which were then used to line the inside of a rapid rotating cylinder drum cut with slits. When set in motion, the static images produced the illusion of moving images like those of a flicker book.

The Victorians were particularly fascinated with capturing and animating images, however the 'invention' of the moving image did not come until some years later, through the work of pioneers such as Eadweard Muybridge in Britain, Thomas Eddison in America and the Lumière Brothers in France. The zoetrope made the move from adult curiosity to child's toy when the American company Milton Bradley patented its own toy zoetrope in 1867.

ALPHABET BLOCKS
J.A. Crandall
USA, *c*.1885
V&A: Misc.60A–1975

KISMET
Produced by Chad Valley/Globe
England, 1895
V&A: Misc.423–1981

Kismet means fate or destiny. This game was intended to show children that by being good and obedient, life would be rewarding. Bad behaviour, on the other hand, would be punished. It has evolved into what we know today as Snakes and Ladders, but as the appetite for moral games declined, it no longer included moral consequences and became primarily a game of chance. Kismet has 42 squares illustrated with moral themes. There are thirteen snakes and eight ladders connecting these squares. The snakes show that wrong-doing and vices lead to punishment, moving the player back on the board, while the ladders lead forward to virtue and eventually, on the final square, to the gates of Heaven. Imagery used for kindness includes attending the bedside of the sick, while faith is depicted by a praying girl. Punishable activities pictured include slander, avarice and selfishness. See also pp.76, 78, 79, 103, 109

MAGIC LANTERN
Designed by Georges Carette
Germany, 1905–13
V&A: Misc.67–1978

LANTERN SLIDE
Manufactured by Gebrüder Bing
Germany, c.1900
V&A: Misc.67–1978

The magic lantern was an early form of projector. It used 'optical glasses' or a concave mirrored glass and an oil-lit flame within a metal casement to project via a lens onto the wall of a darkened room. They were referred to as 'magic' because the pictures seemed to appear from nowhere and the early projectionists kept their workings a secret. The first lanterns were made in the seventeenth century, but they became much more widely available and popular during the nineteenth century.

As well as large lanterns for use in the home or for lectures, several firms produced toy lanterns for children. The slides for this child's lantern were accumulated over several years and include some homemade ones. A large choice of lantern slides were available, from topographical scenes to moral tales and child-friendly fairy and Bible stories. See also p.101

GUS WOODS' PUNCH AND JUDY BOOTH
England, 1912–62
V&A: Misc.19–1968

Punch and Judy shows developed from the characters of the Italian plays of the Commedia dell'Arte, popular from the seventeenth century; Punch's original name was Pulchinello. Versions of the plays toured across Europe, often in puppet form or performed by a troupe of actors.

This booth was used from 1912 to 1962 by Gus Woods of Clapton, together with his assistant, Bimbo. They earned their living giving Punch and Judy shows at the seaside for over 50 years. The booth had to be portable, and despite its large size, it packs away into one canvas bag and a suitcase.

The first known recorded sighting of Punch in England was by the diarist Samuel Pepys in 1662, when he saw a Punch and Judy show in Covent Garden, London. These shows were not originally intended for children, but became popular as a form of family entertainment from the late eighteenth century.

Different variations of the story now exist but the performance generally sees Mr Punch at the centre of a violent and murderous plot. His rage is directed towards his wife and child, and then in defiance of authority towards a policeman. By the end of the performance he cheats the Devil himself. The plot has been popular because of the amoral, physical and visual comedic mischief that Punch causes and gets away with, and despite some level of criticism as to its suitability for a young audience, performances are still popular. See also p.77

SCRAPBOOK
Compiled by Margaret Bolton
England, 1914–15
V&A: B.254–2009

Imaginary play can take many forms. This scrapbook records the made-up Everth family, as compiled by Margaret Bolton as a child. Margaret has used cut-outs from photographs and magazines and some coloured-in images to make her 'family'. She represents herself in the guise of Joy, the book's narrator. As well as pictures of family members, Margaret has drawn extensive plans of the house and grounds, including the colour schemes of certain rooms and stories about what the individuals got up to in her fantasy realm.

In 1915, Margaret's real father died and she and her three siblings were separated and sent to different relatives to be cared for. Margaret may have used this imaginary world and extensive, idealized family as a way of coping with her grief and trauma.

TEA SET
Manufactured by Brookes and Adams
England, 1935–40
V&A: Misc.880:1–1988

Mimicking the actions of adults is a method of developmental learning for a child. Inviting real or imaginary friends or even toys to tea, using miniature crockery or toy tea sets, teaches children about sociability and sharing, as well as simple domestic skills. This tea set is made from an early form of plastic known as Bandalasta ware, which was made by the firm Brookes and Adams in Birmingham. The company produced a wide range of products for the adult market, as well as several versions of tea sets for children. See also p.89

BILLIE AND HIS SEVEN BARRELS
Manufactured by Kiddicraft
English, 1945–55
V&A: Misc.248–1985

Hilary Page (1904–57), the founder of toy company Kiddicraft, developed specific types of toys for children. He spent a huge amount of time studying children at play in nursery schools, and invited ideas and criticism from parents in order to design more effective toys. In his book *Playtime in the first five years* (1938), he wrote about the value of simple toys made from hardwearing materials which could be used by the child to discover play in a variety of sensory forms. Billie and his Seven Barrels is one of the most popular toys produced in the Sensible Toys range by Kiddicraft. Their simple form of brightly coloured plastics, at the time a new and experimental material, invited learning about colour, size and spatial awareness, and due to their modular construction enabled play at different stages of a child's development. See also p.104

PEG BLOCKS
Designed by Milan Morgenstern
England, 1960s
V&A: B.925–1993

Paul and Marjorie Abbatt were pioneers and advocates of innovative and well-designed toys from the 1930s to the 1970s. They believed that play was the necessary work of a child and was vital to social, emotional and intellectual health and development. They sold and manufactured toys as well as being instrumental in setting up Children's Play Activities Limited (founded in 1951) and the International Council for Children's Play (founded in 1959). On a research trip to Vienna in the 1930s, the Abbatts met Milan Morgenstern, who had been developing teaching methods and apparatus for children with physical and learning disabilities. After the Second World War, Morgenstern's designs were produced as a part of the Abbatts' toy range; his pegged blocks shown here allowed for a more stable construction process while retaining a simplicity of form common to his and the Abbatts' designs.

CHILD'S ACCORDIAN
Manufactured by Hero
China, 1960s
V&A: B.92–1996

SHIP'S COMPANY
Photographed by John Drysdale
England, 1960s
V&A: B.243–2009

Playing outside has always formed a large part of a child's development in terms of exercise, physicality and socialization. This photograph was taken some time after the Second World War in an adventure playground set up on a bomb site in London. Adventure playgrounds were introduced to Britain by Lady Allen, a landscape architect, to provide places in which children could play in a physical and imaginative way with no predetermined apparatus such as swings and seesaws. They often contained tools and abandoned objects and gave children responsibility for their own spaces as well as providing play opportunities not linked specifically to gender.

This photograph by John Drysdale is taken from his Adventure Playground series and shows a group of children playing in a rowing boat that has been placed in one of the playgrounds.

LEEDS 1982
Photographed by John Heywood
England, 1982
V&A: Misc.1079–1992

The exact origins of skipping are unknown, but are thought to be rooted in ancient cultures. Skipping and other games of a physical nature were once seen as more appropriate for boys, however, since the nineteenth century, skipping is a game commonly attributed to girls.

There are many different incarnations of skipping, but earlier games tended to involve multiple players rather than one, or as in this case two people turning and jumping one rope. Many skipping games involve chanting songs while jumping, while another popular variation is known as Double Dutch, where two people turn two ropes together in an inwards direction, and the skipper has to keep jumping both ropes in quick succession. As with many traditional outdoor games, the rhymes and rules are determined afresh by each new generation. See also pp.51, 70

HENRY TOY VACUUM CLEANER
Manufactured by Casdon Toys Plc
England, *c.*2008
V&A: B.236–2010

Miniature household toys have been
used for hundreds of years to teach the
developmental and practical skills required
in adulthood. The changing duties
and appliances of adult life have been
represented in domestic toys such as sewing
machines, typewriters, cash registers and
tool kits. The Blackpool-based company,
Casdon, have been producing toys since
1959 and still make miniature toy versions
of tools and appliances. Early examples
from their range include the popular Jumbo
Phone and Super Cash register. During
the 1980s, Casdon further developed their
domestic replicas with the introduction of
branded toy appliances, such as this Henry
vacuum cleaner, allowing children to mimic
the household duties of their parents. See
also p.85

BUMBLE BEE WHEELYBUG
Distributed by HippyChick Ltd
Designed by Wheelybug Toys Pty Ltd
Australia, *c.*2006
V&A: B.248–2010

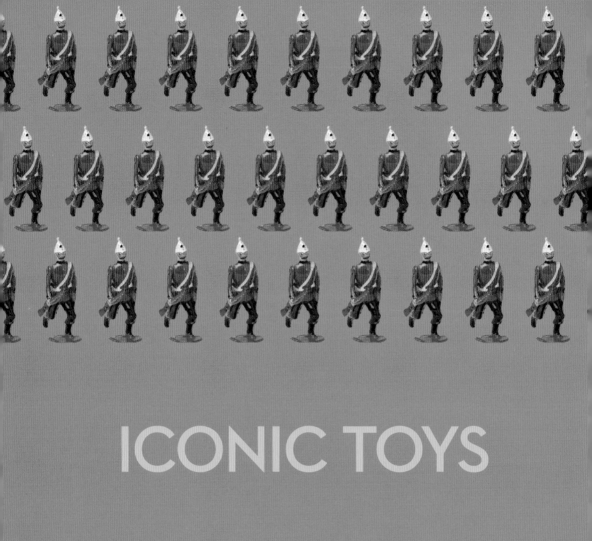

ICONIC TOYS

Good design can create iconic toys, whether in their clear concept, traditional craftsmanship, appropriate choice of materials or an ability to reach a mass market. Certain brands and companies have enjoyed enduring power over decades or even centuries, while others have made their mark with a short-lived fad or collecting craze.

The original meaning of the word 'toy' was a thing of little value, a trifle, and in the past was not automatically associated with playthings or even children: some of the earlier toys in the collection were intended as adult curiosities for the wealthy. Early optical toys, finely constructed automata – clockwork moving toys – and even dolls' houses were intended for grown-ups, before making the transition to the childhood realm. From 1800 onwards, however, the Industrial Revolution, coupled with an increasing demand for childhood playthings, saw a significant increase in mass-produced toys and games for children.

The Museum's game and toy collection ranges from bespoke and highly crafted pieces assembled by master craftsmen and specialist guilds, to the mass-produced and ephemeral. Many toys within the collection have captured the public's imagination to such an extent that they have become minor celebrities in their own right. Teddy bears and dolls can take on human characteristics and often become a part of the family; other toys are simply significant because of their age, intricate craftsmanship or rarity.

Germany has a long and prominent tradition of toymaking in Europe and dominated production until the Second World War. Post-war, production expanded internationally, particularly in the UK, USA, Japan and China. There was an explosion of new materials and manufacturing techniques, such as injection-moulded plastics, and the range and potential for toymaking was huge.

Twentieth-century toys exploited 'famous faces' from films, books and television. One of the first pieces of character merchandise was a stamp case made in the 1890s based on Lewis Carroll's *Alice* books. This was followed by 'celebrities' such as Shirley Temple, Muffin the Mule, Mickey Mouse and the Teletubbies. In more recent years, character merchandizing has become a vital component in the saleability and licensing of a product, and key to a toy company's profits.

PADDLE DOLL
Egypt, c.1300 BC
V&A: Misc.190–1992

This wooden doll made in Egypt around 1300 BC is the earliest object in the collection. It was given by Lady Dale, an archaeology enthusiast, first as a loan and subsequently as a gift to the Museum in 1992. It is perhaps an unusual doll to find in the Museum's collection, because this type of paddle doll was not intended as a toy and is probably not a childhood object at all. In Egypt, dolls like this were thought to symbolize fertility and were intended to be placed within burial sites in order to ensure rebirth into the afterlife. The doll may have been made with hair, which along with the curvaceous shape of the paddle emphasized a womanly shape. The chequered pattern that can still be seen on the bottom half of the doll was probably a suggestion of clothing. See also pp.18, 44, 97, 102

'OLD PRETENDER' DOLL
England, 1680s
V&A: W.18–1945

The Old Pretender is one of the earliest and most famous dolls in the Museum's collection. Dolls from this period were typically made from wood, and few examples of this quality survive. She is dressed in contemporary Anglo-French clothing of the late seventeenth century, including a large fontange head-dress with lappets, and has several highly fashionable beauty spots on her face.

The doll is thought to have been associated with the court of James VII of Scotland (James II in England), based at the palace of Holyroodhouse, Edinburgh. It is said to have been given by the King's son, James Edward, later known as the Old Pretender, to a family of loyal supporters. This doll would have been a highly prized possession, even among a very wealthy family. See also pp.18, 44, 97, 102

Museum of Childhood

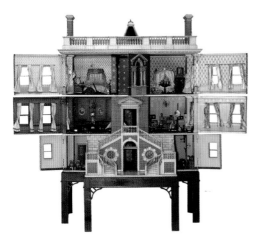

The Tate Baby House was modelled on an eighteenth-century Georgian town house in Dorset and named after its last owner, Mrs Walter Tate. Baby houses – referring to the size and type of house – were particularly popular in Germany and England and were made as status symbols and playthings for wealthy adults to decorate, enjoy and display. Despite its size, the house was intended to be portable and travel with its owner. Even though the house comes apart for this purpose, the relative difficulties of travel by coach and horses would have made this a significant undertaking, demonstrating how important the house was as a showpiece. See also pp.2, 17, 74

MARBLES
Europe, 19th century
V&A: Misc.15–1966

As simple clay balls, marbles have been recorded as toys in Ancient Roman, Egyptian and Aztec cultures. Their simplicity has made them an enduring and adaptable toy, as well as fiercely collected objects to be swapped, admired and displayed. Marbles have been made from a variety of materials, ranging from actual marble to clay to more familiar modern versions in varying glass designs.

Marbles can be used in many games, such as knocking your opponent's marbles out of a circle drawn on the ground or into pre-dug holes. They are also used as gaming pieces in Chinese Chequers and in the 1964 game, Kerplunk! They have proved to be a constant in the changing toy industry, often enjoying a sudden surge in popularity through new trends and fads and as new generations discover them.

BOYS PLAYING WITH SPINNING TOPS
Painted by Richard Morton Paye
England, c.1800
V&A: B.61–2005

SIX MINIATURE SPINNING TOPS
Europe, 1825–75
V&A: Misc.72–1971

Spinning tops came in different shapes and
were an appealing plaything because they
were small, portable and cheap to produce
and buy.

An important requirement for playing with a
top is a clean, dry, flat surface, and the boys
depicted by Paye have found an ideal site in
the paved cloisters of Westminster School.
These types of top were carved from wood
with an internal weight to help momentum;
a string was used to set them in motion.
Other versions have developed using
different materials and methods for rotation.

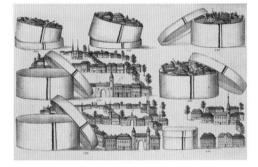

TOY CATALOGUE
Printed for Louis and Eduard Lindner
Germany, 1840–2
V&A: Misc.3–1957

Through much of the nineteenth century, Germany was at the centre of toy production and exported toys widely. Catalogues were a practical tool for salespeople because they were far easier to carry or send than real toys. The first agent known to have produced a catalogue of illustrated toys was Georg Bestelmeier of Nuremberg in 1803, however, surviving catalogues of this age are rare – they were unlikely to be kept when a new toy range and catalogue was introduced.

This beautifully illustrated catalogue of 120 pages is a valuable record of the huge range and price of the toys that were available in the 1840s.

CHESS PIECES
China, 1830–69
V&A: AP.56–1872

Chess is thought to have originated in India. It reached Britain and the West over 1000 years ago, but it wasn't until the fifteenth century that the version we recognize today appeared. Chess is an intellectual and strategic game, based on a war played out between two opponents, with royal, religious and military figures represented as gaming pieces. Played on an 8 × 8 chequered board, different pieces have specific moving characteristics. The aim of the game is to take the King – the most important gaming piece – from your opponent, thus securing his kingdom.

Thousands of examples of these decorative red and white chess pieces were imported from China to England and were very popular with the Victorians, who often kept them under glass domes as ornaments. The pieces all have a carved puzzle base, expertly crafted with a ball within a ball within a ball, typical of Chinese carving techniques.

JEAN QUI PLEURE (JOHN WHO CRIES)
Manufactured by Gustave Vichy
France, 1860
V&A: Misc.19–1970

Automata were extremely popular adult toys from around 1860–1910. In the nineteenth century, the centre for automata production was Paris, where makers such as Vichy and Roullet & Decamps made high-quality examples that were exported internationally.

Here, Johnny the Dunce is seated on a school bench, but is reading his book upside down and is wearing a dunce's cap to denote his stupidity. The hat or cap also has a pair of donkey's ears attached, another symbol of a dunce, particularly in France. Dunce's caps were used within a schoolroom context as a form of humiliation for pupils, and this automaton pokes fun at such figures. When the clockwork mechanism is activated via a key, the music plays a slow, mournful tune, and Johnny moves his head, arms and legs as well as twitching his donkey ears. See also p.39

HAPPY FAMILIES
Published by John Jaques & Son
England, 1860s
V&A: E.870–1950

Standard playing cards have been used by adults for centuries, but children's card games were only introduced in the late eighteenth century and focused on pictures rather than numbers. Popular publisher John Jaques & Son introduced many games, including Happy Families in the 1860s. Card games were already used as educational aids for children, but Happy Families was perhaps the first devised directly for amusement.

These cards were drawn by John Tenniel, who also famously illustrated Lewis Carroll's *Alice's Adventures in Wonderland*. They depict amusing caricatures reflecting the occupation of each family, and include Mr Pots the Painter and Mr Bun the Baker. The aim of the game is to end up with full sets of the same families by trading with the other players.

GOLLY AND DUTCH DOLLS
USA and Germany, 1880s
V&A: B.493-498–1997

In 1895 Florence Kate Upton and her mother, Bertha, illustrated and wrote *The Adventures of Two Dutch Dolls and a Golliwogg,* the first of their thirteen children's books. They were all based on the fictional adventures of the Golly and the Dutch dolls, all real toys that had been owned by Florence when she lived in the USA in the 1880s.

This Golly was Florence's favourite toy and the stories always centred on him as the leading heroic figure.

The Golly remained a popular character and because it was not subject to copyright restrictions, it was widely used in many other stories, including those of Enid Blyton, and mass-produced as a toy and as a logo for products, notably Robertson's jam.

Although many people find the image of the Golly offensive, Florence's doll is one of the Museum's most important objects because it allows us to reflect on historical attitudes. See also pp.18, 44, 92, 102

ROCKING HORSE
Manufactured by P. Leach
England, 1888
V&A: W.38–1946

See also p.14

MECHANICAL TIN BEETLE
Manufactured by E.P. Lehman
Germany, c.1895
V&A: Misc.1–1965

Early production of mechanical tin toys, such as this ornate beetle, was centred in France and Germany. E.P. Lehman was one of the world's most prolific tin toy manufacturers and exported widely to the USA and Britain. From the 1830s, these toys were usually produced by watchmakers, because they involved similar mechanisms, while lithographic printing was used to decorate the tin surface. These types of clockwork toy would have been intended as adult curiosities. See also p.106

Museum of Childhood

GRENADIER GUARDS
Manufactured by Britains Ltd
England, c.1900
V&A: B.115:1–2009

Solid and heavy lead soldiers imported
from Germany dominated the British
market in the late nineteenth and early
twentieth centuries. London-based company
Britains Ltd developed an innovative
production technique for their new toy
soldiers, using hollow moulded lead figures
rather than solid lead, thus drastically
reducing the weight and cost of production.
This technique was essential to their ability
to compete in the market and the key to
their huge success. A good deal of attention
to detail was paid to the figures, including
their scale, proportion and accurate uniforms
representing a wide range of troops from
around the world. Early figures were
handpainted, work which was outsourced
to local women and children near to the
factory in Walthamstow, London. See also
pp.45, 109

LITTLE TOMMY TITTLEMOUSE
Germany c.1908
V&A: Misc.74–1965

The teddy bear was invented in the early twentieth century. The first teddy was manufactured by the famous Steiff Company in Germany and presented at the Leipzig toy fair in 1903.

This much-loved bear, made slightly later, in 1908, is called Little Tommy Tittlemouse. He was given to the collection in 1965, after which his loyal donor would send Tommy a birthday card every year on 24 November until the year of the donor's death, when, sadly, no card arrived. Since this time, members of the public have upheld the tradition of celebrating Tommy's birthday, and on 24 November he still receives cards from all over the world. See also pp.19, 49, 111

SAILOR TEDDY BEAR
Manufactured by J.K. Farnell
England, c.1910
V&A: Misc.14–1974

J.K. Farnell was credited with making the first British teddy in about 1905, two years after the first Steiff bears were produced in Germany. The name 'teddy bear' is commonly believed to have come from US President Theodore 'Teddy' Roosevelt (president 1901–9) who, on a hunting trip, refused to shoot a captured bear. Subsequent satirical drawings of Roosevelt and a cartoon-like bear followed, and souvenir stuffed bears made from plush became known as Teddy's bear. British children may also have related the name to King Edward VII, who was nicknamed 'King Teddy'. The craze of the teddy bear grew quickly, and it has become one of the most popular toys ever made.

This bear was made in around 1910 and has been dressed in a sailor suit with accompanying medals, including the Queen Victoria Jubilee Medal and the Queen's South Africa Medal for the Boer War. See also pp.19, 49, 111

Museum of Childhood

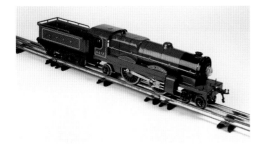

FLYING SCOTSMAN
Manufactured by Meccano Ltd
England, c.1920
V&A: Misc.46–1969

The advancement in different forms
of transport has long been mirrored in
toys; in the later part of the nineteenth
century, toy train sets were being designed
and manufactured in line with the real
developments of the railways. From the
1900s, specific train designs such as the
Flying Scotsman were replicated.

Pre-war, early train sets tended to be large
scale, expensive and luxury items, but from
the 1920s toy companies such as Bing in
Germany and Meccano Ltd in Britain started
to mass produce much smaller sets. These
became hugely popular because they were
more affordable and fitted on the table tops
and floors of modest-sized homes. See also
p.105

MINIATURE TABLE RAILWAY
Manufactured by Gerbrüder Bing
Germany, 1920s
V&A: B.92–2004

See also p.82

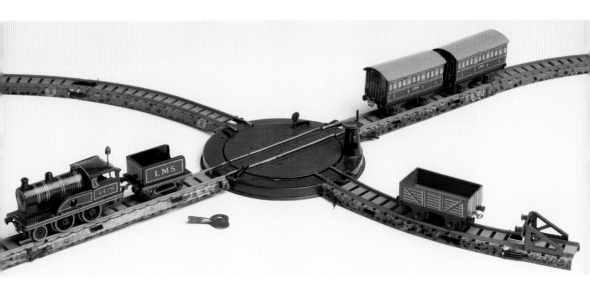

MY DREAM BABY
Manufactured by Armand Marseille
Germany, 1920s
V&A: Misc.36–1964

Dolls resembling actual babies were not produced until the early twentieth century. Before this, dolls were referred to as baby dolls but more commonly represented young children. Marseille produced a wide selection of dolls from the 1880s. There were four different versions of My Dream Baby: mixed race, black, white and south-east Asian, with corresponding features and clothing. This south-east Asian example shows the doll wearing a traditional Japanese kimono and obi (sash).

Ceramic and bisque dolls were hugely popular throughout the nineteenth century, and Armand Marseille was one of the most prolific manufacturers. From the beginning of the twentieth century, ceramic dolls began to decline in popularity, and more robust and cheaper materials such as composition, cloth and, from the 1950s, plastics dominated doll and toy production. See also p.18, 44, 92, 97

SHIRLEY TEMPLE DOLL
Manufactured by Ideal Toy Company
USA, 1930s
V&A: Misc.19–1974

See also pp.18, 44, 92, 97

MONOPOLY
Manufactured by John Waddington Ltd
England, 1936
V&A: Misc.39–1977

Monopoly was first published in the USA in 1935 by Parker Brothers and introduced to Britain the following year. They bought the rights to the game from Charles Darrow, who claimed to have invented it; in fact Darrow based Monopoly on an earlier game called The Landlord's Game, which was patented in 1904 by Lizzie Magie. Monopoly was a huge success and the first 5,000 copies sold out almost instantly. The places and street names chosen in the original version came from Atlantic City, New Jersey, where

Charles Darrow had spent his holidays. Many different versions of Monopoly, now owned by Hasbro, have been produced. These include versions of cities from around the world, a Braille version made in 1970 and Monopoly Revolution made in 2010 to celebrate the seventy-fifth anniversary of the game's launch. Its popularity has never abated, and even today most people are acquainted with its rules. See also pp.76, 78, 79, 81, 109

INTERLOCKING BRICKS
Designed by Hilary Page
Manufactured by Kiddicraft
England, c.1947
V&A: Misc.784–1992

From the 1930s, British company Kiddicraft, led by Hilary Page, and the Danish company Lego, led by Ole Kirk Christiansen, harnessed the process of injection-moulded plastics in the production of their toys. Page set up a separate company, Briplax, to research and develop plastic products, nervous that the market would not accept this 'new fangled' material. Whereas some toy construction kits directly reflected contemporary architectural styles, the use of simple uniform-shaped building blocks conceived by Page and, later, Christiansen, allowed the child to make any number of creative building outcomes. This appealed to a Modernist concept of simple modular design, as well as retaining a clear educative purpose, particularly important to Hilary Page.

The interlocking design of these plastic bricks was revolutionary, enabling the blocks to fit securely together, and allowing quantities of bricks to be built on top of each other. Hilary Page patented his self-locking brick mechanism in 1952, and Ole Kirk Christiansen's patent came later in 1958. Kiddicraft is no longer in operation, having been taken over by Fisher Price in 1989, however the Lego brick is arguably still the most successful construction toy in the world. See also pp.7, 112

MUFFIN JUNIOR
Produced by Moko
England, 1950s
V&A: Misc.362–1980

In 1946 the puppet Muffin the Mule made his first TV appearance with presenter Annette Mills on the BBC's programme *For the Children*. He later featured in *Watch with Mother* and quickly became a household name with his mischievous antics.

The 1950s marked a boom period for children's entertainment, and also saw the huge impact of television on character merchandise and the growth of the toy industry. The company Moko marketed the metal marionette version of Muffin the Mule, called Muffin Junior, so children could play along at home, recreating Muffin's adventures. The puppet was manufactured by expert die-cast toymakers, Lesney, famous for their Matchbox cars.

MECCANO INSTRUCTIONS FOR NO.1A ACCESSORY OUTFIT
Printed by Meccano Ltd
England, c.1950
V&A: B.87:1–1996

In 1901 Frank Hornby patented his idea for a toy called Mechanics Made Easy, and subsequently established the company, Meccano, in 1907. The toy comprised of multiple metal strips with pre-punched holes and a selection of apparatus, including nuts and bolts; with the aid of a spanner and screwdriver, a child could then construct a variety of different moving machines. The concept later grew to include wheels, levers and gears, to teach increasingly complex construction and engineering ideas to children. Ten complete kits, or outfits, as they were known, were available.

This instruction booklet is for an in-between No.1a accessory outfit, which represents a clever marketing strategy from Hornby. This kit would convert an existing No.1 outfit into a No.2 outfit, so that as the child's capabilities increased, so too did the incentive to upgrade your set. Some of the machines that could be built using a No.2 outfit, according to these instructions, include a crane, a drilling machine, a bacon slicer and a punching machine. See also p.101

ROBBY THE ROBOT
Manufactured by Nomura
Japan, 1950s
V&A: B.60–2005

Robby the Robot was a cult figure from the film *Forbidden Planet* (1956), and this toy version was manufactured by the Japanese company Nomura. From the 1950s onward, there was a heightened interest in science fiction, and toymakers took inspiration from the space race and the 1969 moon landing. Japan had been influenced by Germany's traditional methods of tin toy manufacture, and after the war in 1947, under US occupation, Japan resumed exports of their tin toy products and eventually took over from Germany as the market leader, using clockwork and subsequently battery-operated mechanisms for toys. See also p.98

BARBIE TEENAGE FASHION MODEL
Manufactured by Mattel
USA, 1962
V&A: B.72–2010

The Barbie doll was launched at the New York Toy Fair in 1959. She can be seen as a product of her time, reflecting the rise of the teenager, as well as becoming the most famous teenage fashion doll in the world. Her varied careers and roles, from catwalk model to astronaut, aimed to inspire girls to pursue their dreams and aspirations in real life.

Barbie's grown-up and curvaceous look was based on an earlier German doll named Lilli, and remodelled by Mattel. Barbie was perhaps the first doll to cause controversy for directly marketing an extremely curvaceous and unrealistic female form to young girls. See also p.21

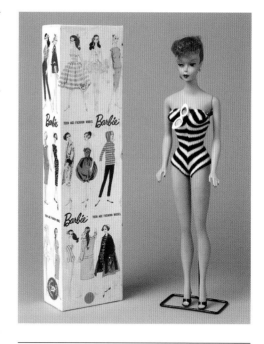

JAMES BOND ASTON MARTIN DB5 CORGI MODEL
Manufactured by Mettoy
United Kingdom, 1965
V&A: B.14–2004

This toy car is a replica die-cast model of James Bond's Aston Martin DB5, which first appeared in the 1964 Bond film *Goldfinger*. The real version of the car was launched only the year before in 1963 and would have been seen as 'cutting edge'.

The toy car came with spy accessories such as hidden machine guns, a bullet-proof shield and opening roof with ejector seat, all features of Bond's car in the film. The combination of film tie-in and secret gadgets made this die-cast toy hugely popular, and it went on to win the inaugural National Association of Toy Retailers' Toy of the Year Award, and Best Toy of the Year for Boys Award, both in 1966. It remained Mettoy's most popular product and is now a prized collector's item.

SPACE HOPPER
Manufactured by Mettoy
United Kingdom, 1970
V&A: B.87–2004

The space hopper was a must-have toy of the
1970s. Said to have been inspired by children
bouncing on fishing buoys floating on the
Norwegian Sea, it was originally patented
in 1968 and launched by British company
Mettoy in 1969. Hopping balls were made
by a number of companies at the time, but
it was Mettoy's bright orange model with
kangaroo-style face that has become a classic
'retro' toy. Redesigned and remarketed to a
new generation in the 2000s, it still keeps its
distinctive and enduring shade of orange.

Museum of Childhood

SCRABBLE, CENTENARY VERSION
Manufactured by J.W. Spear & Sons
England, 1970s
V&A: B.11–2004

Like many of the great toy and game manufacturers, J.W. Spear & Sons began producing fancy goods before moving on to toys. Originally based near Nuremberg, the centre of the pre-war toy industry, post-war the company moved most of its manufacturing aimed at an English-speaking audience to their Enfield factory, acquired in 1932. In 1954 they gained the license to manufacture the American word game Scrabble in the UK. Although the company had a vast range of successful products including puzzles, board games, and craft and construction toys, Scrabble became their biggest-selling product.

The original concept for Scrabble was conceived by architect Alfred Mosher Butts in 1938. It was based on an earlier word game, Lexiko, and was intended to be a mixture of crosswords and anagrams. It was first manufactured in collaboration with James Brunot in 1948 after he had added some minor alterations to Butts' idea. See also pp.76, 78, 79, 81, 103

PROTOTYPE TANK
Designed for Palitoy
England, 1984
V&A: B.2484:1–1999

Action Man was produced by British toy company Palitoy from 1966 to 1984, under license from US toy company Hasbro. With the move to Britain, this iconic action figure had his name changed from GI Joe, but the figures and accessories initially remained the same. Many innovations were made to Action Man by the Palitoy design team. These included the development of a mechanism to create his flocked hair, and a design for a gripping hand so the figure could hold a gun. These ideas were hugely popular and were quickly fed back into the GI Joe range. This prototype vehicle is made from wood, metal and plastic and is incredibly heavy; it was designed for the last Action Man range made by Palitoy in 1984 that never went into production. See also pp.45, 99, 110

AT-AT VEHICLE
Manufactured by Kenner
USA, 1980s
V&A: B.1030–1993

Licensed merchandising perhaps achieved its first truly international success with toys made for the early *Star Wars* films. In the UK, Palitoy manufactured these toys in its factory in Coalville, Leicestershire, under license from US company Kenner.

The AT-AT was one of the biggest vehicles from the film that went into widescale production. AT-AT stands for 'all-terrain armoured transport' and was a transport vehicle for the Empire army, resembling a giant walking creature. It was first seen in *The Empire Strikes Back* in 1980. See also p.109

AMSTRAD CPC464 COMPUTER
Manufactured by Amstrad
England, 1984
V&A: B.166–2010

The first home computer was launched in 1971, and just over a decade later, the Amstrad Colour Personal Computer was a market-leading home machine, along with the Spectrum ZX and the Commodore 64. Games were purchased on tapes and loaded into the in-built tape deck; it often took around twenty minutes to load a game before it could be played. Apparatus such as joysticks made for improved gameplay, and games available for this computer included Scrabble, Winter Games, and Dizzy, a whacky adventure set in a cartoon egg world.

Basic programming could also be attempted. The field of electronics and electronic gaming has been one of the fastest growing industries of the late twentieth and early twenty-first centuries, and products have reached a high level of sophistication. Games are now played by adults and children as individual players, as teams, and online globally with increasingly spectacular play capabilities.

CHAMELEON BEANIE BABY
Manufactured by Ty Warner Inc.
USA, c.1998
V&A: B.183–1999

Beanie Babies were launched in 1993. As with many modern toys, the marketing strategy was very sophisticated – and it led to phenomenal success. Beanie Babies are plush bean bag toys deliberately designed to be affordable and collectible and to fit in the hand or pocket of a child. Vast numbers of different lines were launched in quick succession, which sparked initial interest and then subsequent frenzy among consumers wanting to collect them all. Each Beanie Baby came with a distinctive heart-shaped Ty tag, its own name, a birth date, and a poem. This chameleon, Rainbow, was 'born' on 14 October 1997. His poem reads:

Red, green, blue and yellow
This chameleon is a colourful fellow
A blend of colours, his own unique hue
Rainbow was made especially for you!

See also pp.19, 49, 100

LEGO HARRY POTTER
HOGWARTS CASTLE
Manufactured by Lego
V&A: B.100–2012

The Lego group was founded in Denmark
in 1932 and is now one of the world's
leading manufacturers of toys. Their first
modern construction bricks were patented
in 1958, the design influenced by the newly
developed process of injection-moulded
plastic. From its origins as a simple brick
construction kit, the Lego group has adapted
its products in response to market trends,
such as an appetite for film tie-ins, with
products such as Lego computer games
and this Hogwarts Castle construction set
licensed from the Harry Potter films. This
set comes complete with nine mini-figures
of the film's main characters as well as secret
passages and hidden objects. Key rooms
from within the walls of the magical castle
include Dumbledore's office, complete with
the sorting hat, the Gryffindor common room
and the Great Hall. See also pp.7, 104